A Likely Story

the writing life

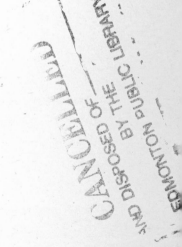

A Likely Story

the writing life

Robert Kroetsch

Red Deer College Press

The Publishers
Red Deer College Press
56 Avenue & 32 Street Box 5005
Red Deer Alberta Canada T4N 5H5

Acknowledgments
Cover design by Susan Lee, The Design Kitchen
Text design by Dennis Johnson
Printed and bound in Canada by Webcom for Red Deer College Press

Financial support provided by the Alberta Foundation for the Arts, a beneficiary of the Lottery Fund of the Government of Alberta, and by the Canada Council, the Department of Canadian Heritage, and Red Deer College.

COMMITTED TO THE DEVELOPMENT OF CULTURE AND THE ARTS

Canadian Cataloguing in Publication Data
Kroetsch, Robert 1927–
A likely story
ISBN 0-88995-103-9
1. Kroetsch, Robert, 1927– —Biography. 2. Authors, Canadian (English)—20th century—Biography.* I. Title.
PS8521.R7Z53 1995   C813'.54   C95-910456-9
PR9199.3.K76Z467   1995

For Meg and Mike and Laura and Dean

"A man never coincides with himself."
Mikhail Bakhtin, *Problems of Dostoevsky's Poetics*

"I am attempting to write an autobiography
in which I do not appear."
Rita Kleinhart, *Chance of Flurries*

"My next novel should be subtitled 'A Likely Story.'"
George Bowering, *Errata*

Contents

A Likely Story

the writing life

Why I Went Up North and What I Found When He Got There

When I was twenty I went up North. I went up North, not to discover gold in the Yukon or to find Sir John Franklin's bones, not even to get rich or to escape from home, but rather because I wanted to write a novel. The logic of that intention seems less evident today than it did in 1948. But at the time it seemed perfectly apparent: I wanted to write a novel; ergo, I wanted to go up North.

Fool's gold is to be found even in the mind. And yet my particular combination of folly and resolve did lead me to encounter the stories that map for us both the North itself and our ignorance of that real and phantasmal place. I did not intend to pursue any of the stories of that place I knew before going there, and yet, even now, by those strategies of recital we call invention, I still imagine I might one day write a novel about the bush pilots who hunted the mad trapper onto the tundra or the men and women who, in the poems of Robert Service, "moiled" for gold—there beneath the northern lights or the midnight sun.

I have a suspicion at times it was that one verb, *moil*, that tricked me into wanting to write and into beginning to write by going North. I should have checked a dictionary instead of applying for a job; to moil: to work hard, to toil, to slave.

Writers are, by any definition, slow learners: they cling to the happy illusion that to write will be to avoid work. "The men who moil for gold," they read in a poem, and they are touched by the mystery of its sound, untouched by its signification. They are prime candidates for any trip into the North. To write is to step or stumble over the edge of the known into that category of desire that defines itself, always, just a hair's breadth short of fulfillment. To write is, in some metaphoric sense, to go North. To go North is, in some metaphoric sense, to write. One goes North at that very point on the page where the word is in the process of extending itself onto the blankness of the page. Whatever inscription might exist behind the point of the pen, there can only be blankness ahead.

What I have to say from here on is impossible to say; therefore I must say it. It is precisely that uneasy relationship between the word and its intention, between the word one is writing and the space that will contain the word and threaten it with erasure, that constitutes the northward swerve. The enduring impulse of European culture is the impulse to go westward, with latitude unwavering.

To go North is to slip out of the fastenings of night and day into other versions of light and dark. I don't know how to explain this. I do remember, however, an Inuit woman in Aklavik who trusted me enough to ask one summer evening if it was true that, farther south, darkness actually fell in the middle of a summer night. What I remember most intensely is that I hesitated in answering: there, north of the Arctic Circle, I was no longer sure of the answer. I had swerved away from the Western world and its secure sense of the structure of time.

But already I digress. Back in the spring of 1948, when I knew clearly my intention, when I was about to graduate from the University of Alberta with a Bachelor of Arts degree in English and Philosophy, I applied for a job as a laborer on the Fort Smith Portage, on the southern boundary of the Northwest Territories.

The sheer folly of this will be clearer if I remind you that in 1947 oil had been struck near the town of Leduc, just a few miles south of Edmonton; wiser young men than I knew where to head.

But I wanted to write a novel, and to write that novel I knew I must head North.

The logic of youth has a reckless validity. There seemed no other possible way for me, at the time, freely to make the beginning I felt I had no choice but to make. I suppose the trick is, often, to match a sense of destiny to a sense of the individual and heroic act. We come in these latter days to the questions: Is the author dead? Did the author write the text or did the text write the author? And I take these questions seriously—I am still uncertain as to how much we are the creators of the North and how much we are the creations of the North. Insofar as the North carnivalizes given Canadian assumptions—turning upside-down assumptions about time, about direction, about urban ambition, about America—it seemed an escape from the authority of tradition and hierarchy, an escape that would allow me to become a storyteller.

The North was a silence that desired as much to be spoken as I desired to speak. It was the very geography of my desire. It was the landscape of my unspeakable narrative intention.

But that North desired its silence as much as it desired to speak. I understood that condition one afternoon in Inuvik when I was standing with an old Inuit man where not only the houses and the over-ground sewer lines were under construction, but the very streets themselves. He had expressed some resistance to that invasion, and I asked him what it was he disliked most about the town that had been designed and was being built to fit uneasily the eastern shore of the eastern-most channel of the Mackenzie delta.

"The noise," he said.

I had hardly noticed the noise. Surprised into silence, I heard the numbing roar of machines, the drone and clatter of machines.

Living on a riverboat, one came to hear the sound of the marine engines as a lullaby. I would wake up at night when the engines went off. In a camp on shore, one came to take for granted the sound of generators and their engines and their numbing insistence.

To that Inuit man who had spent a lifetime on the tundra, there was hardly such a thing as silence, only significant sound; noise to him was of another race and another culture; it was quite possibly the destruction of what he took to be the world's story.

I conceived of the novel, back in 1948, as the direct transport of experience onto a page. I went up North to have the necessary experience; the novel would take care of itself.

Perhaps I wasn't entirely wrong: perhaps I err now in entertaining the possibility that the novel is a shaping of experience in terms of elaborate codes that are not only literary but social and psychological and phenomenological as well. Perhaps I stray from error into heresy in entertaining the suspicion that to write a novel is to shape the absolute of writing into a fiction of experience.

But back then, in 1948, I did get hired by the Yellowknife Transportation Company, and early one morning I went out to the Edmonton Municipal Airport and walked up to a small bush plane and asked the man loading cargo into the plane if the pilot was around.

"I am the pilot," the man said.

Early that morning, with the sun of the temperate zone on my neck, with two brand-new pencils and two pads of blank paper in my duffel bag, I delivered to that airport an innocence colossal in its magnitude.

As you have guessed by now, I proceed here by willful digression that instructs the novice against the illusion of knowing.

One sunlit night in Tuktoyaktuk, a white woman told me with innocent wonder that she'd just met an old Inuit woman who wore in the pierced flesh between her lower lip and chin two buttons of bone. That same white woman, behind her camera—we were both at the time looking at and avoiding a team of sled dogs that was staked out and apparently starving on the shore of the Arctic Ocean—wore pinioned in each of her pierced earlobes a piece of tin and plastic artfully shaped to look like a parrot.

But I was telling you how I went out to the Edmonton Municipal Airport to catch my first flight into the North. Late that afternoon, flying toward Waterways, which in my mind was not only the end of the railway system but also the end of civilization, we hit low cloud cover.

I say late afternoon even though I had arrived at the Edmonton airport early in the morning. If there is a single act that characterizes life in the North, it is the act of waiting. One time in Inuvik I waited six days for a plane that would take me to the Yukon. I have never—not yet—been to the Yukon. One time at Axe Point I waited forty-five days to take a shower. By the time the water system was in place, I'd developed a kind of heroic resistance to the idea of taking a shower; I'd gotten into the northern tall-tale tradition whereby hardship is the badge of sourdough status. On the riverboats, we waited for days in the spring (or at breakup—in the North there is a fifth season) for the ice to go out, then for the ice to clear its own channels down the river—the northern rivers flow, perversely, toward their own immobility. In the North, people wait through whole seasons for freight to arrive; they wait years for governments to make decisions; they wait decades, or possibly centuries, for treaties to be signed.

To wait is to alter violently the momentum and purpose of Western culture. A condition generates its own system, its own values, and waiting becomes an alternate culture that is rich in reflection and meditation, those forms of inaction that become versions of action; waiting is a recovery of the eternal into our obsession with linear time. And in that waitingness, the body itself adapts, finding itself contained paradoxically in a version of space that is at once intimate and vast.

But as I was saying—flying, there, toward Waterways, we hit low cloud cover.

Again, in the way of the North, the pilot—Art Bell I believe was his name—was not licensed to fly above the clouds. That is, he was not licensed to fly by instruments; he was strictly a pilot who flew by the eye, who mapped his way by sites recognized. If you have ever looked down on a northern landscape that is more water than land and surely a study in the eye's confusion, then you will appreciate that my innocence and my illusion of knowing had found their accomplice, and we might have been going North together, the landscape and I, to write a novel.

Art Bell flew his small plane into the Athabasca River valley and stayed just above the water, just under the clouds, between the riverbanks. I suppose he didn't have enough fuel to take him and us back to Edmonton. Certainly no profit was to be made in turning back to Edmonton. And there was no way we could turn around.

After what seemed to me and the two other passengers, who had suddenly been revived from what seemed the most fatal hangovers on earth, Art Bell looked back over his right shoulder and remarked casually, confidently: "We're going to make a jump here, up over the bank. I think the landing strip is right up there." He tapped the long steel drive shaft of a diesel marine engine that reached from the airspeed indicator back to the rearmost 100-pound box of no-longer-quite-frozen boneless beef. "Try to get behind this thing if you can," he added.

His sense of concern was touching, almost unmanly, given the macho situation we had bargained our way into.

Before I could scratch out a will on my first blank pad, using one of my new pencils, the plane did indeed jump. Straight into the cloud cover.

And there, not so much under us as straight ahead of us, through the jack pines that in some way caressed us toward our destination, was a stack of fuel drums that could only signal the presence of a landing strip. I was up North.

We waited for two days in a beer parlor in Fort McMurray until one afternoon Art Bell, who had glanced once every half hour through a small window at the heavy sky, announced mysteriously and for no apparent reason, "I think we can make it now."

The process of recollection is never easy. I seem to have no recollections at all of my first arrival in the Northwest Territories. What I do recall is my second arrival, the time when I went North for a second season: we landed at a place on the Mackenzie called Axe Point, and when we landed, a dog team came onto the landing strip. On the sled was a young Dogrib boy who had accidentally shot himself in the right armpit. The gaping hole was stuffed with filling from a mattress. Once we'd unloaded that bush plane, the boy was lifted on board and the pilot agreed to take him to Yellowknife on what was called in those days a mercy flight. The landing strip was soggy and muddy, and the pilot had to race down that landing strip three times before he finally got airborne.

But to go back to my first arrival, the arrival that I do not remember at all: strangely, I remember more clearly an arrival I'd planned, then rejected: I might, in the week when I arrived for the first time in the North, have been arriving in Europe.

A first cousin of mine, while serving in the Canadian Army in Holland, had been billeted with a Dutch family and had fallen in love with the family's oldest daughter. He was in the process of arranging for us to get a free trip to Europe on a cattle boat when I learned that I'd been hired to work as a laborer on the portage at Fort Smith.

Freight going north down the Slave River from that last train station in Waterways had to be off-loaded at Fitzgerald, then trucked something like twenty-five miles past a series of spectacular rapids, then loaded back onto barges at Bell Rock, north of Fort Smith; from there the tugboats could push and tow the loaded barges all the way to Tuktuk on the Arctic coast.

There are rival formulas, rival narratives if you will, for the writing of a first novel. Back in 1948 it was still assumed that one should get on a cattle boat and head for Europe and once in Europe make one's way, if at all possible, to Paris.

How I managed to avoid that particular formula is, again, lost in low cloud cover; and believe me, I have never been one to fly by instruments. Perhaps I sensed that the model offered by Pound and Eliot, by Fitzgerald and Hemingway, was singularly out of working order—though I do confess, almost blushingly, that my generation still believed strongly that one should go out and have *experience*—and that mostly of a mean and miserable sort that involved, as it did for Jake Barnes in *The Sun Also Rises*, coming back with a few scars and a story appropriate to the scars. I might add, parenthetically, that I got myself a lifelong back injury by tossing boxes of frozen boneless beef out of a walk-in refrigerator to a deckhand who claimed he couldn't lift the boxes by himself; this was in Fort Good Hope. It may be that an aversion to cattle and cattle boats led to my injurious encounter with frozen beef. It is more likely, I would guess now, that the return of thousands of young men from Europe with stories to tell made me in secret and in silence turn to the North for the silence that would let me tell stories of my own—and I had not yet learned the curious ways in which the stories one tells are not ever and cannot be one's own, especially not stories of the North. There is, for the novelist from the South going into the North, an unnerving gap between the story one wishes to tell and the story one is hearing.

I recently found on one of the pages in one of the pads I carried North a list that maps the North as beginning from Waterways, a list that measures miles of travel by water. For me, now, it is a kind of found narrative, a cryptic narrative that let me map myself into that unknown:

from Waterways:
Saline 25
Tar River 46
Bitumont 54
Sled Island 70
Poplar Point 95
Point Brule 105
Whitefish Creek 155
Jackfish Creek 155
Willows 170
Fort Chipewyan 187
Little Rapids 209
Peace River 215
Caribou Island 277
Fitzgerald 287
Fort Smith 303
Big Eddy 468

Resolution 507

Wrigley Harbour 612

Providence 660

Pipe Cache 687

Axe Point 700

Head of the Line 750

Fort Simpson 816

North Nahanni 926

Wrigley 968

Fort Norman 1120

Norman Wells 1170

Sans Sault Rapids 1235

Fort Good Hope 1293

New Chicago 1343

Thunder River 1418

Arctic Red River 1507

Mouth of the Peel 1542

Fort McPherson 1561

Aklavik 1661

What I do remember from my first arrival in the North is my first morning of work on the dock at Fitzgerald. We were unloading boxes of dynamite for the gold mines in Yellowknife. I was put to work with a huge métis by the name of Gabe.

He was a native of the area, and yet I soon discovered that he was as much of a stranger in that camp as was I. Gabe was the first person about whom I made my few sparse notes, after working twelve- or fourteen-hour days—slugging freight or bulling freight; we had a choice of verbs, both of them close to moiling. I was young; I liked working there on that dock's edge where the river worked swiftly along the pilings, beginning its surge into the first white water of the rapids.

Two Bavarians were in that camp: Tony and Alfred. Alfred was an ironist and Tony was a true believer. They were men in their late fifties, exhausted from years of manual labor in bush camps and on the docks. Alfred, the ironist, was fond of saying of Tony, "Tony has been in Canada only nineteen years, and already he owns two blankets."

The slippage was there, somewhere, between the word and the intention, the dream and the reality.

If the North American quest westward is in its many disguises a quest for Eden, the quest northward is the quest for the secret passage to that unimaginable place, the Indies. Going North, we join Sir John Franklin and his crew. We join with those who would not venture into the Americas, but around them to a world of spices and tea and silk, a world of untold riches, untold adventures. And in that search for the Northwest Passage, in that turning north to seek westward, the word *untold* becomes the amassing and the disintegrative word.

I wanted to write a novel.

Perhaps Tony and Alfred recognized in my last

name an origin I did not myself know, and they were
trying to warn me clear of disaster. But my first notes
were not about those two Europeans who had reversed
the journey to Europe that I had planned and then
avoided; my first notes were about Gabe. I cannot tell
you his last name because I was sure I would never forget it and didn't write it down. "Gabe," my handwriting
insists in my notes—though I have no recollection of
the writing—

>   *Gabe—trapline 40 miles long—3 cabins 15 miles
> apart—he goes to one—stays for 2 days and traps—goes to
> the next and next—then visits each again on the way back—
> he is out for two weeks at a time. In the fall he stocks each cabin
> with wood, food and dog feed. He carries only his bedroll. He
> travels with 5 dogs. Once made 62 miles in 5 hours. Usually
> takes 3 hours between cabins—depends on trail and dogs.*
>   *He is going to fish this winter. There is a lake in his trap-
> ping area that is full of whitefish and trout (some trout up to
> 30 lbs). He is going to fish through the ice with his six nets,
> and once a week a McInnes plane will come in and take away
> the fish—they buy them right off the ice at 4 cents a pound.*
>   *Gabe has a cabin by his lake—60 miles southeast of Fitz.*
>   *He made $1,100 in 19 days this spring—beaver and
> muskrats.*

He was from a hunting and gathering society, and
in a way he was profoundly different from the people I

had known most intimately, the citizens of a farming community in rural Alberta, where I'd spent most of my childhood and youth. Perhaps we were the enemy, always, the farmers who by their farming made the city possible and life stationary, and we were overtaking the hunter again.

Gabe was the first person in that camp to strike me as a lesson in something, I knew not what; perhaps I had myself, in going North, reverted to hunting and gathering, trying to pick up a story after failing to grow my own (and I was a dismal failure at farming). Like all our ancestors, I had become migrant again, moving with the seasons, with the weather. Gabe was easy and uneasy, there on the river's edge, the open water in front of him, the forest behind him. I asked him what to do about the mosquitoes. He told me to ignore them. I asked him why he didn't live in the bunkhouses with the rest of us. "Too much noise," he said.

I was quiet again. Silent. I was learning a lot about silence there in the North; and I had gone intending to make a beginning at sounding the story. What I first saw, or found, was not a beginning but an end.

Gabe did not know, but his eyes knew that his way of life was under sentence. He was a seasonal laborer on a dock that was about to be shut down because of the completion of a highway to Hay River, a road that would take freight directly to Great Slave Lake, avoiding the series of rapids at the Fort Smith Portage. The first of those rapids, in all their beauty, with pelicans lifting from the rocks, was called the Rapids of the Drowned, not after an Indian legend, but after two priests who had come from France intending to bring Europe to the trappers who lived on the muskrat season and the caribou season and the plentiful supply of fish—two priests who had gone out in a canoe to try their hand at fishing.

I was tempted to return South. It says in my notes that the old steamboats, going upriver from Fitz to Waterways, burned 180 cords of wood on a trip that took three days and three nights. If you didn't get wind bound on Lake Athabasca. But I had missed the last passenger boat, the last sternwheeler; that had given way to the diesel tugs and the airplane. And I had just sufficient knowledge of bush flying to make me want to stay on the ground for a spell.

It was not Gabe, but rather a young métis woman who one evening introduced me to the local graveyard. The freight barges, windbound at the western end of Lake Athabasca, by their not arriving gave the whole camp a free evening. Perhaps I asked the young woman to take me to the graveyard; there is, suppressed somewhere in my story, a trace of the Romantic quest, the solitary hero, the unsung song. If you can't get born, at least you can die with a certain flourish.

Each grave site in the overgrown graveyard was surrounded by a small picket fence that had once been painted white and had once, or did still, wear at its head a small wooden cross. That métis woman explained to me that the Indians would not eat the berries, the saskatoons, the chokecherries, the high bush cranberries (mooseberries, she called them) that grew so plentifully in the graveyard because, obviously, they contained human blood, and if you ate those blood-full berries you would die within twenty-four hours.

I didn't believe her. And yet, I didn't eat any of the berries. I had come somehow to recognize that I was there as sympathetic transgressor, but a transgressor nevertheless.

Before I go on to talk about Jewel—and that was her real, as well as symbolic, name—I should mention another graveyard.

Two seasons after meeting Jewel I made my first visit to Aklavik. While there, I went to the grave of Albert Johnson.

Johnson, too, was a trapper. But he had been a white trapper and not a man from the hunting and gathering societies of the North; he was an interloper. He was a transgressor on Indian traplines.

Albert Johnson, the mad trapper, the madman of Rat River in Wilf Carter's song, the man who shot a Mountie dead, was a hero of my childhood. The pursuit of Albert Johnson was reported on radio; back in 1932 it was one of the first instances of the use of radio to follow the high and, by now, clichéd drama of crime and pursuit. I recall hearing of the Mountie who died and of the Mounties who pursued the silent trapper who refused to give so much as his name to his pursuers—even his name is conjecture. He was hunted by dog team, and he was hunted from the air by the famous bush pilot Wop May. He deceived the posse, escaped—and then turned around and walked back into their trap.

Albert Johnson was both story and artist for me—this, before I went into the North. He wore the silence of the artist like a badge, an indication of his will toward self-destruction. In his transgression he lost his name to his story; he was the death of the author. He was not the story I wanted to write. But he was a clue to that story. And then I got to the place, I got to his grave site.

On a riverboat, sitting in the galley over a cup of coffee makes up a considerable part of what passes for adventure. Fellow adventurers at that table are likely to swap stories. There in the galley of the M.V. *Sandy Jane*, I began to hear new versions of the story of Albert Johnson. In my notes for 1950 I've written:

> Some say he wasn't a bit insane. A greenhorn Mountie made an investigation and got himself shot.

> Some say he thought he was shooting a Hare Indian who was robbing his trapline.

Some say the police shot an unidentified man and called him Johnson just to make the case look good after losing so many men.

Some say Johnson hired a man to make the run for him. He had a lot of money and offered this man a large sum which he could have if he escaped. Then Johnson quietly disappeared.

I had gone to the grave site to learn something and had learned little, and all the while the men who shared the galley table were telling a story by having it unravel into stories. We learn by learning slowly. What I had to learn from graveyards I had already learned in Fitzgerald in my first season on the river, in the company of a young métis woman who was, as I now so vividly remember her, the most beautiful woman in the world, a lost Helen for whom no Paris had crossed the inviolate sea.

This woman's name was Jewel. You may recall that the young woman who plays so important a part in the later life of Lord Jim in Conrad's novel is named Jewel. I had gone North with Conrad's novels in my head, if not in my duffel bag.

The young woman was my age almost to the day. In contemporary parlance she would be called a hooker, but to the men in that camp she was something else. She was, in Conrad's phrase, one of us. She was something of a legend; in one day in a mining camp near Yellowknife she had made $500. But like the rest of us, she had very little to show for her moiling for gold.

She worked in the small restaurant that served the settlement, an unpainted wooden structure that didn't have a sign out front because everyone in the settlement knew what every building was, insofar as buildings have identities—the church, the Hudson's Bay Company store, the log houses back in the bush, the fancier house that belonged to the HBC factor. There were no police in that settlement. The RCMP were in Fort Smith at the other end of the portage. I believe we had a weatherman in residence, for whatever reason.

Jewel lived in two small rooms above the restaurant. I was not one of her paying customers. I was quite simply in love with her, and in a way I think she loved me, and we went for walks that included not only the graveyard but the gate of Wood Buffalo National Park, where we actually did one evening see a herd of buffalo.

I suppose I must at this point explain that while she was in a sense a whore, I was without equivocation a virgin. How I had attained to this ideal and maintained its integrity a few weeks past my twenty-first birthday is a matter for spiritual and psychological speculation not appropriate to this occasion—something to do, possibly, with an Alberta background and the health propaganda of World War II, which insisted that any sexual activity whatsoever would lead directly to the loss of the offending member. What interests us here are the metaphoric possibilities of the occasion:

the young would-be author about to encounter, in some Joycean sense, experience.

The men of the camp were, to a man, one night gathered elsewhere to listen to a heavyweight boxing match on a radio and to drink beer. The restaurant was empty of all customers. I was not terribly interested in the outcome of the fight; even then I had about me an inability to deal with violence.

Jewel and I, on a pretext that I no longer recall, went up from the empty restaurant to her two small rooms. To name the event the loss of virginity is surely to misname what can only be regarded as a gain. What I remember with great intensity and a kind of reverence is not the moment of that happening, but rather the moment when I knew the happening was about to happen. I was, truly, then, the novelist, knowing above all else the phenomenology of desire.

What I remember is not the event, but rather the "gaze" that preceded and forecast and accepted the wondrous inevitability.

There was a mirror on Jewel's tall dresser. We had not glanced at each other, she and I; such is the nature of innocence, even in its moment of surrender. Such is the nature of conspiracy. And we did not directly glance at each other; rather, our glances met in or through the reflections of ourselves made available by the mirror's delicate inversions. By our very indirection, by our avoidance, we gazed directly into each other's eyes.

I need hardly distract the attentive reader with the details of what happened next. Let us proceed at once to the metaphoric implications.

We had remained wordless, Jewel and I. We had not spoken. We did not speak until we returned to the empty restaurant below and I asked for a glass of water.

I was offered a glass of water.

I accepted the glass of water, and I drank a sip, carefully, from the full brim.

As I have suggested, my recollection dwells on the moment when I knew the happening was about to happen. I understood, lucidly and insanely, for a moment, that Jewel and I would, however briefly—and it was briefly—dissolve the whore–virgin dichotomy that so painfully blocks the story Western civilization wishes to tell itself.

The North makes possible a new story. It makes that story possible, not through the encounter with the self (held dear by Western thought), but rather through the astonishing encounter with an Other that eradicates self into all its disparate potential. I was become the possibility of the us that is me.

Instead of leaving the North, I hired on to become a purser on one of the riverboats that ran from Fort Smith north, down the Slave, across Great Slave Lake, down the Mackenzie to the Beaufort Sea.

On my first trip north from Fort Smith, we ran all night. And all night we could watch, on the eastern shore, a forest fire that burned vividly, creating in the night a horizon.

I am not suggesting a metaphoric reading of that fire. What shocked me was its literalness; it was a fire burning through hundreds of square miles of forest, a fire that would burn unfought, unchecked, until a river or rain or winter stopped it.

It was a night journey, too, that shaped this last of my encounters with the telltale Other in the North.

This time we were sailing out of Fort Providence, just below the outlet where the Mackenzie leaves Great Slave Lake on its long slide down to the Arctic. It was late fall, the water was low, darkness came early onto the river, so early that we had to run as late as possible; in the morning there might be dense fog for hours.

Since I was purser, I had little to do on board the M.V. *Richard E.* while we were traveling. Often, I went up to the pilothouse and sat with the pilot. The landscape had become a kind of hero to me. And, beyond that, I sometimes read the landscape against what I had read of it in Alexander Mackenzie's journals. What caused me to marvel was not the truism that said little had changed since his trip, but rather my sense that he had recorded so little of what was there to be seen. In his will to find the Northwest Passage, he had been too intent either to shift his sense of time or to learn by waiting.

I dawdled in the pilothouse. At the height of summer there was no night to travel in. By early fall we were matching the last delivery dates on freight against the formation of ice on the decks of boats and barges, around docks, in the mouths of tributary rivers.

I had become a friend of our chief pilot, Vital Bonnet Rouge, a Dogrib from Fort Providence who had spent most of the summers of his long life on riverboats on the Mackenzie.

We were going downriver, and we were about to run the Providence Rapids. Darkness was falling fast. We were pushing four barges lashed in pairs ahead of us. Because we were going with the current, our speed increased as we began to be swept along by the water pouring into the long stretch of rapids.

Those are not white-water rapids. The water is clear, coming out of the lake; the pilot must read all depths in the shadows and boil spots that show on the racing surface.

I was sitting on the counter behind the wheel, and Vital was hardly taller than the wheel when he stood behind it. I was sitting on the high counter along with the logbook, a pair of binoculars, and empty coffee cups. From my perch I could see out the windows on all four sides of the square pilothouse; we were running with all lights except the running lights out, so the pilot could see more clearly. It was past dusk, into early darkness, a time when shadows are extremely deceptive on a river.

We were about to make a sharp and treacherous turn across the apparent direction of the river's flow, a turn that was necessary to keep the boat and our four barges in a deep but narrow channel.

"What's that shadow over there?" Vital asked.

I told him it was a rock, hardly believing he didn't know. I thought he was, in some Dogrib version of humor, teasing me; he liked doing that.

But a moment later he asked again, of another shadow, "Is that the big rock?"

And it was then I realized he couldn't, in that variety of falling darkness, see clearly. His sight was failing him. We were going through the Providence Rapids on the basis of his memory. A pilot was not a pilot without a memory of 1300 miles of river as they might be navigated, downstream and up, at different seasons, in different water levels, in different kinds of weather. It meant having a knowledge of place that was as absolute as disaster. Every lobstick or gravel bar or sandbar or cleft in the skyline of spruce and jack pine was a sign to a pilot. Every shade of water meant something; every boil spot in its drift and violence spoke a language.

But we had hit the Providence Rapids exactly at the time when Vital, because of his failing eyesight, had to rely on a kind of sixth sense: the complex elaborations of his memory. But even to do that he had to have a fix on a landmark.

He rang the engine room and slowed the engines. I

became, for a long half hour, his eyes. I told him what I thought I was seeing; I was into the North and of the North, and I was reading the landscape as if my life depended on it. And possibly it did. We entered into a small conspiracy, Vital and I. The members of the crew who weren't in their bunks asleep or in the engine room were in the galley, drinking coffee. Vital and I, in the dark wheelhouse, became the language of ourselves. To put it most outrageously: we became our version of lovers. He moved small and silent in his moccasins, his hands quick on the wheel. I had to describe to him what I saw: a world of shadows, shifting patterns of light and dark, the possibilities of a rock ledge, a gravel beach, a channel.

The river, I learned, was a shifting narrative of itself. Vital and I were swept into that narrative, and yet, once there, once we were inevitably and unavoidably there, we had to write the narrative, too. We had to write it, and we had to write it together. I was there, new, without memory. Vital was there with a memory that needed the bald landmarks of my seeing. His hands climbed in beautiful precision up and down the handles of the wheel. We broke the silence with my few speculative words, the sound of the chains translating the skill of his hands into a shift in the boat's rudders.

When we were safely through the rapids, into a wide and slow channel again, Vital began to tell me stories. He said nothing about our trip through the rapids.

He had never told me any Dogrib stories. I had been too ignorant to know the Dogrib Indians had a cosmology of their own. He told me stories of his people, stories I don't remember now.

He was, somehow, giving stories to his novice writer. He was offering me stories. But he had already given me the story I had been looking for. He had shown me how to move through the slant and recurring passages that are the quest of northward journeys. He had shown me shades of unknowing; he had let me see that even the pilot who knows it all must sail with a kind of reckless care, a kind of humble listening to voices other than his own.

I wanted to write a novel. Vital Bonnet Rouge, there, in the Providence Rapids, had welcomed me into the North, had welcomed me North. I had waited and I am waiting. But I was, for that swift moment, in the falling dark, in the moving water, in the quick of our careful breathing, there. And I had been taught a writing.

I Wanted to
Write a Manifesto

I became a writer many times. One of the first times I became a writer had a great deal to do with my not being tall enough to see; I had to reach with my right hand, blindly, into a holy water font.

I want to explain this in some detail, partly because that small and readerly gesture was somehow transformed into a writerly gesture, partly because I began then, unwittingly, to know the connection between "hand" and "manifesto."

I'm troubled that I cannot begin to guess how old I was at the time. My difficulty is this: I lived on a big farm that employed in those days a lot of hired help. That was in the early thirties; my mother had as a hired girl an unemployed school teacher. That woman, at my mother's suggestion, taught me how to read and to write at least in an elementary way.

The trouble developed when, at the age of six, I went to school. My cousin, Orpha O'Connor, a grade twelve student, came to live in our house and to drive the horse and buggy in spring and fall, the horse and cutter in winter, the four and a half miles to what we called a "town school," in Heisler, Alberta.

There were three rooms in the school, four grades in a room; things had to be done in order and without exception. The teacher, Miss Boyle, in what we called the first room, took an immediate and considerable dislike to me, because I knew how to write and how to read. I upset her system.

In order to restore her scheme of things to the world, I pretended not to know how to read or write; and thus I learned all over again how to do both. I learned both twice. As a result, I am uncertain what my age was when I entered into the alphabet. I do know that Miss Boyle had brilliant red hair, and in the course of my life, I've had a series of relationships with red-haired women in which I've tried, sometimes by feigning and deferring, sometimes by self-erasure and self-mockery, to please each and every one of them.

Even now, under the pressure of mere memory, I hear my language threatening to disintegrate.

It was my grade twelve teacher, in the city of Red Deer, Alberta, who told me I should make a career of writing, and never for a moment since that late afternoon when I stood by her desk in the failing winter light—the only student left in her home room, the only boy who ever lingered after class—never since she said, "You're always writing. Why don't you become a writer?"—I was seventeen—have I for a moment doubted how I must spend my life.

The war was on, it was a January day in 1945, and up until then I'd been unable to decide whether to become a fighter pilot or a sniper. The metonymic leap from that indecision to my accepting a destiny as a writer seems difficult to explain unless one takes into account the color of Mrs. Aylesworth's hair. Her hair was a brilliant red.

As I was saying, I don't know how old I was at one of the first occurrences of what might be called my writerhood, but I was small enough so that I had to reach up beyond the level of my eyes to dip my fingers into the font.

The font in the Wanda church was curiously high; it was a basin made of a block of streaked white marble, mounted on a tall white pedestal. In a way the tallness of the pedestal for the holy water font seemed a compensation for the sorry state of the church's steeple.

The Wanda church was one mile straight south of our farm; you could see it from our kitchen windows. There were no hills or rises, no trees, in that mile of distance, no buildings. The church was called a mission church, the priest and his "home" church were in the town of Heisler, in the opposite direction from our farm.

The Wanda church got off to a bad start. It did not in fact have a steeple at all, because after the square wooden tower was built at the front of the small wooden church—the tower that became the vestibule on one floor, the choir loft on the next—the farmer who had agreed to put up the money for a pointed and shingled steeple decided he was no longer a believer. He'd had no idea how much steeples cost.

As a result of his change of heart he was killed in a farm accident and his wife went mad. She became a witch who chewed gum a lot and then put wads of gum in quart-sized sealers because she knew the devil was trying to get hold of some of her spit.

A cousin of mine, one night, driving his team and rack, having worked on a threshing crew all day, having lingered over a late supper and a couple of glasses of chokecherry wine, saw lights in the choir loft of the flat-topped tower. The church wasn't wired for electricity. Since there were no vehicles of any sort in the churchyard, he drove closer to investigate, and lo and behold he saw a circle of devils dancing naked in the choir loft. He whipped his exhausted horses into a gallop and never once looked back.

That same cousin, Leo was his name, worked often for my father, and one summer my father had Leo and another man, a Swede, busy digging a well near the pig barn, which was a long distance from our horse barn and our main yard and our drilled well. A dug well, you understand, is quite a different matter from a drilled well; you expect to hit a different kind of water.

In the minds of most of our hired men, I was considered to be hopelessly spoiled and hopelessly lazy. The two men digging the well, sweating in the cool, cramped space beneath the casing they built as they dug, drank up all their drinking water. I made the mistake of dropping by to see how they were doing; I somehow wanted to be on hand when they struck an underground stream and had to step up onto their ladder.

They gave me their empty water pail, a Rogers' syrup tin with a wire handle on it, and told me to go to the well up in the main yard and bring them back a pail of water.

The walk to the barn was long and tedious, and I was being asked to interrupt a busy life of my own, even if I had appeared to be doing nothing. I felt a certain resentment.

I went to the windmill by the water tank and held the pail under the long trough. Our well was famous for its good water; farmers came a considerable distance to get drinking water from our well.

I filled the pail, and then, for whatever reason, I urinated into it. Just slightly. Not enough to change the color or the taste of the clear, sweet water. But I urinated into the full pail. When I delivered the pail to the two men, I told them, I said, "I peed in the water."

"You didn't," the Swede said. He was standing on the ladder, reaching out of the dry well to take the pail from me.

"I peed in the water," I said, again.

"You did not," my cousin Leo said, from down at the bottom of the well. His voice had a kind of an echo-y quality about it, coming from down there.

The two men took the pail and drank the water, and I marveled that men are so impervious to truth. They carry with them the paradigms of their claims to the world, and no mere words will deter them from believing. I had by this time entered school and learned twice to read and write. I went on hunting blackbirds with the slingshot I'd made (I never hit a single bird, ever), and I meditated not on my supposed offense but rather on the nature of language and its relationship to behavior. I was dumbfounded that those two well-diggers had placed so little faith in the very language they had used to command me to perform their disruptive and odious little chore.

Only years later was I struck by the smaller irony of their digging a well and dying of thirst while doing it. At the time, it was the failure of my plain speech that troubled me; I was experiencing a Wittgensteinian anxiety. What devices of rhetoric, I asked myself, in a rudimentary way, of course, might have persuaded those two men that I had peed in the very water they were so determined to drink? What strategies of narrative and discourse might have persuaded them to go fetch their own pail of water?

I became a writer many times. Another time had to do more explicitly than the well incident with sex, though to this day I have a suspicion my peeing in the water had something to do with a phallocentric view of the universe and my boyish unease at hearing it annunciated. The two men, I should, in a readerly gesture, tell you, struck water at something under twenty feet; the water proved to be too hard for human consumption, but okay for pigs.

But before we get on with the incident relating to sex I should further elaborate my belief in the efficacy of language.

That Sunday morning in the Wanda church when I walked toward the holy water font I was both young enough and old enough to have a trust in what I had learned, and I had learned that holy water was well water that had been transformed by a ritual blessing. It had been transformed by the priest's words. Words were all the priest had to work with, except for a minimal motion of his right hand, raised in a gesture that I might now see as writerly.

He, of course, while making the gesture, while speaking, wore on his face a look that signified further a transformation of the face in the too-brief moments of

47

our—to use the exact word—coming, those moments when a benign holiness and a profane translation coincide.

I once took elaborate pains and spent considerable money in order to gaze upon the ecstatic face of St. Theresa as represented in marble by Bernini. There, that day in Rome, I was not disappointed. I felt a mixture of envy and terror at the prolongation of her moment of unutterable joy. Pierced by the spear of her martyrdom she comes to a moment of knowing that will last as long as stone might last.

The prairies of the West were surveyed into blocks that measured two miles from north to south, one mile from east to west. The road allowances ran around these rectangular blocks. This meant that a person living in the middle of the west side of a block had to drive three miles to visit someone living in the middle of the opposite side of the block, one mile away. As a result there developed fascinating and unofficial trails across the middles of those blocks of land.

I lived in the middle of one side of such a block, and a family of my favorite cousins lived on the opposite side. The trail across the intervening land ran through a quarter section that had never been broken; a homesteader from the American Midwest had bought it from someone, probably the CPR, had gone home for the winter and not returned. As a result there was in the midst of my experience a quarter section of unbroken sod complete with buffalo grass, with myriad wild flowers, with sloughs surrounded by willows and poplars that so teemed with birdlife that to this day I have recurring dreams of those perfect, round sloughs and the varieties of birds that made them loud.

Some distance off the prairie trail that wound across this land—my father rented the quarter and fenced it and ran cattle on it—was a boulder. What is called an erratic.

It had been transported hundreds or even thousands of miles by glaciation, that boulder. I remember exactly what it looked like, and yet it cannot possibly have looked the way I remember it.

I repeat the pronoun "it" in a futile attempt to deny the rock its sexuality.

In my exact memory it is a composition of pure and erotic curves. Lying where it did in the buffalo grass, it invited my darkest complicity. At its highest, at what I must call the inverse swoon of its top curve, it rose almost as high as my waist. You must abandon all your assumed notions about boulders. That rock was smooth without being shiny; its remembered color reminds me of the bodies I have seen on the curved, lubricious, hot beaches of Greek islands, those buttocks and shoulders and breasts, fresh from morning flights out of Brussels, out of London and Stockholm and Frankfurt, no longer white, not yet red. At the time—and I remember I was twelve years old in that crucial summer—in my infatuation with language that summer, I might have risked the words *roseate, damask*.

My cousins hated the words I was using, that summer. They were slightly ashamed of me. They accused me of having swallowed a dictionary. Their attitude was reason enough for my not completing my journeys across the virgin field.

To make a long story short, that rock became both the conspirator and the participant in my first adult love affair. I was at the time too young and incompetent and lazy to be put to work in the fields; I was old enough to recognize that I was shamelessly and ferociously fired by sexual desire.

I became quite literally aroused at the sight of that rock. My hands were sufficient journey, and I reached for universes of grass and stone. Not I—*we*—touched. We knew a rough and blind joining; we knew the bereavement of separation. We found our lovers' talk and found, also, the limits of all words.

When I first saw the round stone that is supposedly the world's omphalos, there in Delphi, I knew, secretly, it was the trace of an outrageous love. When I first saw the Venus of Willendorf, there in that enormous museum in Vienna—when I first saw that small, carved stone, buttocks and belly and breast exaggerated, face mysterious, I knew again our long and human and inhuman inheritance of desire and the place of rock itself in that base wish to go not up but down.

The priest in the Wanda church was a man named Father Martin. If he had a first name—a Christian name, as we used to say—I don't know what it was. In a community of German Catholic farmers who had come together from Ontario and various states in the American Midwest, he was not of German origin; he was born in England, shipped off as a small child to grow up with relatives in Canada. That's the story I heard. He was a much loved priest, in part because he avoided any activities outside his priestly role. Where I was considered dreamy—*RPK*, I was sometimes called, in efforts to startle me into the world—he was considered preoccupied, devout.

Father Martin was a kind of artist of the impossible, and when he blessed holy water, I knew it was blessed. He knew what he must do—and didn't bother himself with questions. One time when visiting home, I asked him about a priest who was a friend of his. "Oh, Father Hickey," Father Martin said. "He's in Rome now. Studying theology. Whatever that is."

I don't think Father Martin ever troubled himself about that exquisite, small block of marble that was the basin of the holy water font, there in a modest church where plaster of paris was the stuff of statuary. He knew what he must do, and when the power to bless overtook him, he was his gentle and resigned self, soft of voice, almost smiling.

After I left home and went away to take grade twelve and listened to Mrs. Aylesworth and tried to write a few poems, I thought often of Father Martin and his mastery of ritual speech and silence.

One of the poems I wrote was about a Japanese samurai. I wrote the poem in the spring of 1945 when Germany had surrendered but Japan had not. Even now I can quote the last four lines of that poem, and I cannot quote from a single one of the poems I have written since. It ended:

> *The wise old moon very knowingly frowned*
> *On the man who lay sprawled on the cold gray ground.*
> *He had taken the law of his Maker as vain,*
> *And now he lay broken, inert, inane.*

I was troubled by that poem. I am duly impressed now by the variety of stress patterns I was able to manage. But even then, at the age of seventeen, I was troubled. And I was troubled because the poem had not let me write the poem I wanted to write.

This is what I'm trying to explain. To you. To myself. This is why I wanted to write a manifesto.

You see, I did not at all want to write a poem about a Japanese samurai. To be, briefly, frank, I'm not quite sure I know what a Japanese samurai is. I'm not so sure

I knew then either; it must have been something put into my head by the rhetoric of war and its adjunct, hate, and I am not a very good hater, ever.

Mind you, I did not want to write a love poem either, because I did not want my family to find out about the affair with the boulder.

I had written a poem, a pretty fair poem, to all appearances, and yet I was horrified, thunderstruck— because the poem contained a variety of elements that violated my every intention as poet.

I knew, or I had learned from Mrs. Aylesworth, that the appearance of the moon in a poem was in all probability bad news. Further, I was dead against personification and other versions of anthropomorphism (prejudices I've long since abandoned), and I was more inclined to see cheese than wisdom in the moon. And yet, there in my poem was a moon, a wise moon, and a frowning wise moon at that.

Somewhere in what I so admired and loved—somewhere in the generosity of literature—was a tyranny that was making me write a poem that I did not want to write.

I did not want the hero of my poem to die at the end of the poem; I guessed that any samurai with half his wits about him would live to see another day and to fight another battle. Yet there lay my hero in the last line of the poem, "broken, inert, inane."

I was, at the age of seventeen, in reaction against

my Catholic boyhood, and while I was willing to conceal my apostasy and radical agnosticism from my four kid sisters, I was damned if I'd mention the Maker anywhere in one of my poems, let alone have Him show up at the end and dole out His version of justice and generally steal the whole show.

I was troubled by what the idea of a poem—by what the poem of a poem—had made me say. I was being forced by the shape of the poem, even by the language, to say things I did not want to say.

I fear we must go back for a minute or two; the chronology of the self makes a variegated coat that just barely covers the soul.

I mentioned earlier my cousin Orpha O'Connor, who drove me to school when she was in grade twelve and I was in grade one and learning to read and write for the second time. Orpha was not a topnotch student but she was quite simply so beautiful that a number of the older boys in school—all the boys, I'm tempted to say—were willing to kill each other for her attention. I may have forgotten to mention that Orpha had quite attractive auburn hair. Those older boys took to cornering me at recess, down in the school basement or out in the school barn; they took to asking me complex and unorthodox questions about Orpha, on the theory that proximity makes for knowledge, sometimes using a vocabulary with which I was not entirely intimate—and without quite understanding the questions or knowing the parts of the body to which they referred I must answer on pain of death.

We become writers in various ways.

The incest taboos were rigorous in Heisler, and I only barely loved Orpha myself. I suppose I hear now, in the mysterious syllables of her name, a feminine version of the name of that fated poet, Orpheus; I see in her name faint anticipation of my own going down into that very place called the underworld. But the point I am making is this (and in my youth I identified with Orpheus himself and the death-dealing gaze of the poet; now I identify with Eurydice, fearful that the asshole up ahead might look back): the power of language over the poet is life granting and fatal.

I wanted to write a manifesto.

Love and hate are not always the contraries they would seem. One time I was having two glasses of beer in a shabby beer parlor in Wainwright, Alberta, when an old man sitting by himself across the room signaled me to join him; for some reason he looked familiar, and I walked across the beer parlor floor as I had walked toward the holy water font in the Wanda church, years earlier. As I approached the old man's table he said, "Aren't you Bobby Kroetsch?" "Yes, I am," I said. I had less difficulty then with ontological questions than I do now. "I used to work for your dad," he said. He hesitated. I signaled the slinger to bring us four—I raised four fingers over my head, with the thumb across my palm. The old man went on. "You were," he said, in a voice that still harbored a trace of loathing, "the most spoiled brat I ever saw in my whole life."

His expression "my whole life" had a finality about it that humbled me. Ed Basil was his name (I've used his last name in a novel; I believe I turned him into a priest); he was something like Robert Frost's hired man; he drifted around the prairies, showing up at our farm when harvest was done and jobs hard to find and wages falling. I paid for more beer, and we talked. He couldn't believe that just that morning I'd received my first acceptance, ever, for a piece of my writing. The word "acceptance" casts a curious shade. I was going to receive twenty-five dollars on publication. The story was called "The Stragglers."

There I was, my first acceptance in the right hind pocket of my jeans, and my first reader was, in a way, that ragged old man who wouldn't let me change my story. He said I was spoiled rotten by a mother who led me to believe I had a destiny to accept rather than a life to endure. He was that kind of philosopher.

I'll tell you one thing more about Ed Basil. He caught a freight that night. We drank ourselves foggy, and then we walked over to the train station, and somewhere in the shadowy dark, he let me help him as he gave an awkward jump and roll at the same time, and he lay on his back on the deck of a flatcar. I had wanted to go with him for a ways. I'd wanted to have the experience, but I couldn't do it. I don't know why I'm telling you this.

But I was talking about a poem. One of the first poems I wrote. When I read that poem and wasn't happy and wanted to write a manifesto instead, I was somehow reminded of a Sunday morning in summer when Father Martin blessed enough plain water holy to see his small congregation through a year.

Summer went. Fall came and went. We were into the depths of a prairie winter, and still the supply of holy water was unstintable.

The Wanda church was empty all week long and unheated, which meant that early on a Sunday morning in winter a local farmer had to arrive early and go into the crude basement—a hole dug in the ground; as I recall I describe that basement in *What the Crow Said*—and light a fire in the inadequate furnace. He had to stoke up enough of a poplar wood fire to keep the parishioners from freezing stiff in the forty-five minutes it took Father Martin to say mass.

On the particular morning of which I speak the church was bitterly cold. The furnace hardly warmed the four pew ends that butted on the grate, fitted into the floor in the middle of the aisle. Father Martin's breath froze as he spoke; he set something of a record, even for him, for getting through a mass that included at least a brief suggestion of a sermon.

As we were leaving the church it was the custom to dip the naked fingers of one's right hand into the holy water font and to make the sign of the cross while hurrying through the vestibule and beginning to talk to one's friends.

I pulled my right hand out of an overcoat pocket—we wore overcoats then, not parkas—and reached up to dip my fingers into the holy water.

Or rather—I tried to dip my fingers into the holy water.

You, dear reader, in your contemporary skepticism—and I feel sorry for you at this moment; I feel pity—you have already guessed what I am going to discover.

To my utter astonishment, the holy water was frozen.

In that instant, at an age which I cannot now reconstruct, I was launched into a crisis of belief from which I have probably never recovered. I could not see into the font. But I discovered the contents of that marble basin as a reach of unshimmering ice, a sloughlike landscape of scorching cold, a typological forecast of the frozen lake I would find, years later, at the end of Dante's luminous portrayal of the Inferno.

I discovered the betrayal that is at the heart of language. In that terrible instant of my childhood I realized that the priest's blessing, Father Martin's words, the words of that saintly man whom I admired even if I did not ever want to become a priest, had not rescued ordinary water from its ordinariness.

I glanced in blunt horror at the adults around me. I suppose in all truth I go on glancing in horror at the adults around me. Unflinchingly, there, they touched their fingers to that bowl of ice; they made, each of them, more or less, a hasty and perfunctory and desert-dry sign of the cross.

Did I myself make the sign of the cross?

I don't remember. Somewhere between the moment when I reached up and into the holy water font and the moment when I should have commenced the making of the sign of the cross, I entered into a secret dialogue with a strange and uneasy voice that turned out to be my own.

I hasten to add that for all of this, I am something of a happy person. But not too happy.

Did Father Martin know he had not succeeded in transforming the ordinariness of the water in that font? How could he have that realization and still go through with the process of its transformation? My questions were not in any sense theological. What troubled me, there, that bitterly cold prairie morning, outside that small white wooden church on the snow-white fields, was more literal: How could water that I had taken to be exempted from the mereness of my world turn out not to have been exempted at all?

My greatest temptation, always, has been, not the

temptation to disbelieve, but rather the temptation to believe. What, then, is the nature of the fictive enterprise?

I realize that right here and now I should come clean and tell you, lucidly and without equivocation, what I have for years been trying to do as a writer. I did believe, and I do still, in public intention and public declaration. What else is a manifesto all about? Why else write what can only sound like autobiography, when I do not believe the autobiographical is possible?

This is a bit like going to confession. And I caution you that I used to, as a boy, make up sins so the priest wouldn't think I was lying.

I used to confess to using bad language. I thought, through most of my childhood, that using bad language meant making errors of grammar and style.

Somewhere around 1979 I flew from Winnipeg to Minnesota to give readings in Milwaukee and Minneapolis. As the readings fell, I was left with a Sunday free.

My mother's parents moved from St. Cloud, Minnesota, in 1901, and homesteaded in Alberta; my mother was born in the then District of Alberta in 1903. I remembered vaguely that my grandfather, George Weller, long dead, was supposed to have a surviving sister in St. Cloud. We referred to her as Aunt Rose, though in fact she was my maternal grandfather's sister, the last survivor of a family that had numbered into the teens.

Perhaps I did what I did because I wanted to hear of a soldier's heroic life; my maternal great-grandfather was wounded while serving in the Union Army during the American Civil War; he refused to have a shattered leg amputated and spent a year healing himself and limping home from the battlefields. Perhaps I was fooled by my Aunt Rose's name; I expected her hair to have a reddish tinge, a henna hue.

I caught a bus out of Minneapolis around mid-morning on a late winter day. As it turned out the countryside was white with melting snow and the air was full of fog; I saw nothing on the entire ride.

When I got to St. Cloud I looked in the local phone book and found a list of people bearing Aunt Rose's last name. By a stroke of luck I found myself talking, on my first call, to a granddaughter of the aunt I was seeking.

I had to do some tall talking to explain who I was. Then I had to explain why I was, after all the years of my—so to speak—genetic departure, back in town.

"You won't want to meet Aunt Rose," Thelma said. My distant cousin turned out to be named Thelma.

"I must," I said.

"She's in an old folks' home," Thelma said. "You won't want to meet her."

I should have remembered the well-diggers and their

blind insistence. But I learn slowly and late. Instead I said, again, "I must. Really."

Thelma was playing poker and drinking beer with three other women, a Sunday ritual they had engaged in for years, right after early mass. It was obvious, when the cab dropped me off at her house, that Thelma was less than happy to see me. She was about my age. She didn't invite me through the door; she told me to wait outside and backed her new Toyota out of the garage.

Visiting hours were not yet begun. Thelma and I were led by a nurse—allowed by an unwilling nurse— we were disturbing her scheme of things—down a corridor of the old folks' home and then to Aunt Rose's room.

Aunt Rose was lying on a pink chenille bedspread on a metal-frame bed. She had hardly any hair at all. She was nearly bald. She had a few teeth, apparently, under the whiskers and folded skin of her mouth.

Thelma explained to Aunt Rose at length and repeatedly that I was a grandson of her oldest brother, George, the brother who married a Warmann girl from next door and took his unsuspecting bride off to the District of Alberta.

"Unsuspecting bride" is my expression; it was not Thelma's.

"I came here to talk to you," I said. I said that to Aunt Rose. I felt that Thelma was doing a bad job of communicating, and I wanted to help out. I felt I had to shout. "George was my grandfather. Your brother George. I am George Weller's grandson."

Aunt Rose opened her mouth. She had no teeth at all. Her tongue moved small and shadowy, far in the depths of her mouth. She opened her mouth, but she did not make the slightest sound. She seemed to be struggling to utter a sound; she said nothing.

I had traveled to her bedside to recover my own history. But it was only I who could speak; she could not say a word in return. I don't know if she recognized me; I have these epistemological anxieties. I like to think that once, for a moment, she tried to nod. Once her fierce dark eyes glowed a small connection.

For some reason I thought of Ed Basil—or perhaps I only think of him now—hopping a freight. I think of my dead samurai, inert, inane.

Only when I was on another bus, returning to Minneapolis to give a reading in a famous art gallery, did I realize I had been given my own history.

Aunt Rose's mouth was a nest.

Her mouth was the recurrently mute sign of all my days. It was the possible sign of nothing. It contained and offered the shape of all nothingness. It was, however, at the same time, the rock in the field to which I had walked and from which I had not wanted to return. It was the disconsolate cry I had heard from my own throat. It was the holy water font.

Aunt Rose might have spoken and in the act of her

speaking silenced me. Instead she had given me the open flower of her mouth. She gave me the sphinx of her mouth. Her mouth was the perfect circle by which I encountered everything I thought I had left behind. It was the riddle that I must offer my answering into.

The spittle on the gray lips of Aunt Rose's mouth was not even sour to my kiss; it was as sweet as water.

We are always too young to be old, too old to be young.

When I set out to write a story or a poem, or a love letter—or, for that matter, a postcard—I approach again the door and exit, there in the biting cold of a prairie winter morning, in the Wanda church. I am that small boy, in a brand-new overcoat that marks and embarrasses me as a privileged child, and I reach one hand over my head, beyond my line of vision, toward the water in the font—toward that open mouth of water.

Again, I reach. And in the mixture of knowledge and self-deception and innocence that is each of us, I assure myself . . . this time, I say . . . surely this time . . . at least this one time . . .

Blindly, I trust. I reach. And again I am surprised by the tips of my fingers. Again I am surprised—into the impossibility of words—by the perfect and beautiful ordinariness of water.

And I have written my manifesto, after all.

The Cow in the Quicksand and How I(t) Got Out: Responding to Stegner's *Wolf Willow*

I arrived on the prairies twice. One time I was, as the verb has it, delivered; one time I motored on my own. I was born in Alberta in 1927; I drove into Winnipeg from Upstate New York in an aging green four-door Dodge Dart in 1978. By that duplicity I might have wished to gain a surplus of perception. Accidentally, I inherited two deaths.

Design and accident combine in our writing of this landlocked and skylocked terrain. Just fly from Winnipeg to Regina or to St. Paul, watch the mapped land and the movement of clouds.

When I was a boy drinking Orange Crush in the Canada Cafe in a small town in Alberta, the farmers who had eaten dinner (the noon meal) sometimes offered to flip a coin and to pay Wong Toy either double or nothing. What I remember is the terror and elation that I, a listening boy, felt at the speaking of that wager. I remember neither the winners nor the losers.

Double or nothing somehow became the wager by which I might live a prairie life. I recognized even then how hard farmers—and also the chinaman, as we called him—worked for a living. They did not work for money, they worked for a living. That, too, was a lesson. And I wondered at the mystery of their working so hard by design and then risking so much to chance.

They wore the weather close to their skin, those prairie people. Rain and drought and hail and snow— the varieties of weather had a way of riding out of the farther west on the same horse. "Double or nothing," the farmers said. I liked the way the coin leapt off the flicked thumb, spun high in the ferocious light, hesitated. You had to make your call while the coin was still in the air.

A careful misreading is one of my rules; it makes for creative errors. I was a writer for a long time before Dennis Cooley wrote "Fielding," and yet when I read that text I recognized in it a prior text that had enabled me to write. Time is another peevish mystery on these Great Central Plains. I quote at length from Cooley:

> I remember you
> years later
> bent in the white heat
> on our 55 Massey
> dragging the discer

over Evendon's section 7 miles north of town
its plates glinting on the rub of dirt
and the loud scrape of rocks
grinding off sparks
your engineer's cap ruling the red
across your forehead
and the startling white softness of your body
underneath the gray cotton shirt you always wore
and the smell of soap and cream
you pulled through the zipper of
your leather shaving kit
on Saturday nights and how
the heat losing its dirt edges fast
we rolled down the gravel road
over the big hill under
the orange slant of sun
with Hank Snow blowing us down into Estevan
from CHAB in Moose Jaw yellow
on the radio of our '53 green Ford

Just to think it could be
Time has opened the door
And at last I am free
I don't hurt anymore

and how the mercury-vapour street lights
would take us in their blueness past
the forkclinks and the lemonhalibut smells

fanning from the Canada Cafe
direct to the onoffonoffon incandescence
drawing us
dreaming down into
the violet of the Orpheum theatre
where for 15 cents we witnessed
Gene Autry the singing cowboy
rescuing flickering women
in black shadows

"I remember you," Cooley begins this section of his poem for and about his father, and in the blur of pronouns we let ourselves or we welcome ourselves into the poem—or we are seduced into its small and overwhelming journey, and time disintegrates softly.

His Canada Cafe was mine; I know that for sure. His. Mine. I. . . . We are in that landscape and from it; we share a climate, a history, a set of conditions social and cultural and economic that carry us into a narrative of Saturday night in a prairie town.

Or is it a narrative of how place is turned into poem? Or is it, to be more reckless, a narrative of the father, the lost father, himself rescued in the guise of forlorn women? And why do we flinch with pleasure, hearing those lines, "the startling white softness of your body / underneath the gray cotton shirt you always wore"? And what is the connection between that figure at work in the fields and the trip "into the deep violet shade of the Orpheum theatre"? And who among us dares the singer's task? Or the singer's journey to the land of the dead?

To be a writer one must be, whatever else, a reader. One recognizes in texts the doubles that allow the writing self into the recognitions that become words.

I'm going to proceed by responding to a book that I in a sense read before it was written, then read again after it was written. That is one of the advantages of bargaining oneself into a maze of wins and losses. "Matching," we called it, strangely, there in the Canada Cafe. *Matching* to see who would win, who lose. And of course one hopes that Orpheus will make the attempt once more to rescue the dead bride—even if one is oneself, like Cooley's Fielding, that missing person.

Or to reverse the coin—perhaps the gaze is all we have that is special to us, as writers in this landscape. Language comes after; language is an announcement of deathly consequence. To begin to write is, already, to accept loss.

The 49th Parallel is a line. A line of writing. That bizarre name suggests at once an abundance and an absurdity. Like most names, in its very claim to exactness it wins enormous power. The Medicine Line, the Sioux said. Don't cross that line, we say, desiring at once safety and transgression. Or: I'm going across the line today, we say in Winnipeg—to shop for cheap booze in Grand Forks.

By a paradox that inscribes and erases that line, a quintessentially Canadian text was written by a quintessentially American writer. In 1955, Wallace Stegner published a book called *Wolf Willow: a History, a Story, and a Memory of the Last Plains Frontier.*

The subtitle announces our temptations. We are tempted to write a history, with all its claims to authenticity, to validation by research, to generalizations that assert themselves as truths. But against all that we know—as lovers know each other—the temptation to tell a story. We know the impulse to exaggerate the ramifications and the delight, to leave out where leaving out speeds up the plot, to clarify the hero by a reckless but admirable spending, to separate good from bad by summary execution.

A memory, Stegner says. Against both history and fabulation, against both the supposed exactness of history and the artifice of story—not a memoir, but a *memory.* Against those larger and intimidating designs looms here, in our landscape, the astounded and the astounding voice of self (and I invite you: read Tom McGrath, read Lorna Crozier, read David Arnason or David Williamson or Patrick Friesen or Jan Horner or Di Brandt). We as readers listen, and in our listening we hear the prairie/plains strategy that pretends against all pretension in its simple claim: but I was there.

Stegner wrote his book out of a long absence and a brief return. Born in 1908, he was a child on his parents' homestead in southwest Saskatchewan from 1914 to 1920; writing of that place as a "middle-aged pilgrim" he could say: "Our homestead lay . . . right on the Saskatchewan–Montana border—a place so ambiguous in its affiliations that we felt as uncertain as the drainage about which way to flow."

Ambiguity, Stegner cautions us, at once "gazing" from a distance and standing close, is one of his themes. Sometimes to name is to possess; sometimes a dictionary is the catalogue of our hesitations.

When I was a boy, living in the parklands and not on the true prairies at all, we children in spring used to strip the outer bark off a branch of silver willow and chew the sweet, stringy inner bark and believe that winter was over. The taste of the bark of that willow—silver willow, wolf willow—says to me what the smell of its leaves said to Stegner: this is the various place we call home.

Stegner offers a huge and difficult generalization about us prairie dwellers. He begins his book by talking about "the drama of this landscape," and he goes on to say, "It is a country to breed mystical people, egocentric people, perhaps poetic people."

It is no accident, and a happy accident, too, that Stegner makes us uneasy with his use of the verb *to breed.*

By design or accident, we have found in the image of the horse the dramatic juncture of sky and earth; in novels as widely different in content and intention as

Sinclair Ross's *As For Me and My House* and Sharon Buta-la's *The Gates of the Sun* the horse figures our predica-ment—and reminds us that the novel had its beginning in another landlocked and open landscape. Don Quixote, in the country that apparently gave the horse to our landscape, gave us the story of Don Quixote, his feet not quite on the ground, his head not quite in the sky.

"It is a country to breed mystical people. . . ." And while I am not quite sure I know what mystical means, I have a suspicion I believe what Stegner says.

Mysticism, as I feel the word in my bones, has something to do with whatever it is that can't be fully articulated. As a prairie writer I've committed myself to speaking the unspeakable, and *unspeakable* here is a pun. My Aunt Mary told me not to say what I was saying. My critics ask me what it is I'm trying to say.

I'm talking about our very unwillingness as well as our inability to speak the name of all that we are. I'm reminded of the claim that, during the Dirty Thirties, farmers stopped naming their farms—because the names made the farms too easy for money collectors to find.

Our strategies, even when we claim to tell the God's own truth, are strategies of evasion. We are so often trying to slip out of the grip of someone or something. I won't attempt to name that someone or something, but in the metonymic slithering of the world it might appear briefly as a tornado, more enduringly as a political leader.

We who are from Minnesota and North Dakota, from Saskatchewan and Manitoba, share not only a set of borders but also a variety of temptations, of alibis, of curses placed upon our minds and bodies, of outrageous joys, of furtive pleasures. I'm not attempting here an examination of place. I'm asking how the plains or the prairies enable us to recognize ourselves as writers, then enable us to write.

I should caution the reader that I'm renowned for my ability to misread the question—even my own—and for my ability to answer the question by indirection, misdirection, deferral, delay, rhetorical dodges, postmodern artifice, sexual innuendo, and just plain outright lies.

I find it fascinating that even so realistic a novelist as Sharon Butala, a hard-boiled rancher from Stegner's own "last plains frontier," sees in our landscape and in the drama of that landscape the figure of Coyote. Perhaps to be mystical, in our world, is to have doings with the trickster.

But then, consider the opening of Butala's *The Gates of the Sun*, published thirty years after the appearance of *Wolf Willow*. This is from the first opening, the opening in italics that is a dream and contradicts its dreaming:

He remembered a river, wide, flat, silver. It went on forever in every direction and far off from where he stood. People in miniature boats bobbed on its surface, without purpose or direction, like leaves on a puddle. Or rose and floated in the sky, above the water's surface, on a silver streak. Had he dreamt it, perhaps? No, somehow they had crossed a river and he had clung to his mother's black-gloved hand.

And three paragraphs later:

The journey, as time went on, tumbled out of a confusion of sensations to a series of clear and bright, but disconnected pictures: the long, jolting ride on the hard wooden wagonseat, the instant when his mother's hands were larger and reddened in the sun, the horses' flanks tightening and releasing. And the green of the Cypress Hills.

I'm willing to call this mysticism, this description of arrival, once more from across the line, in the green of Stegner's Cypress Hills.

There is so often something apocryphal about our stories. They are secret stories. They stand outside our own canonical notion of what the story should be. They are, in ontological ways, of doubtful authorship.

In a prairie/plains world that insists by daylight that we are perfectly sensible people, the stories come as mysteriously as the horses to young Andrew Samson in the second opening of *The Gates of the Sun*. In that opening he is awakened from dream by a sound.

He steps outside the shack in which he lives with his mother:

> *The full moon struck him, froze him in its white light. . . .*
> *They came into view. An endless herd, flowing past, through the*
> *unfenced, undefined yard, an immense herd of horses split in*
> *their flow by the house, the barn, the corral, so that they were in*
> *front of him and behind him, approaching on one hand and*
> *leaving on the other.*

Butala gives us those two matched and, at the same time, different openings. The flow. The dream become reality, the reality become dream. The definition and the resistance to definition. Cooley's father's Orpheum. The mysticism. We are of two minds.

More recklessly and dangerously, Stegner suggests this is a country to breed egocentric people.

In what sense egocentric? We writers pride ourselves on our sense of the tribal. Margaret Laurence, Mark Vinz, Rudy Wiebe, Aritha van Herk, Bart Schneider, Sandra Birdsell, are only a few of the names that come to mind. We dream of knowing the extravagances of tribal union implicit in Robert Bly's *Sleepers Joining Hands*.

But *egotistical*, Stegner insists. And perhaps he means that in the absence of traditional culture and its elaborated implications we fall back on our own experience. Stegner writes: "However anachronistic I may be, I am a product of the American earth, and in nothing quite so much as in the contrast between what I knew through the pores and what I was officially taught."

When I read those lines, at the University of Iowa, in the home state of Stegner's mother—when I read those lines I knew I was reading the credo of my own discontent. I was at the time a graduate student, studying the tradition that I had somehow to learn to appreciate; and I was learning from Stegner that I had to learn, in the process of accepting the tradition, how to resist it. I knew that I, too, Canadian, was a product of the American earth, and there in those square and sensible buildings, on the banks of a small river, surrounded by beautiful fields of corn, inhaling the air that all summer long stank to high heaven of pig shit—and to this day I stir to that smell, thinking wild thoughts of Transcendentalism—there, I began to understand the saving grace of, and the insistent need for, the egotistical.

Let me tell you a story.

And by the way, Stegner is exact to the point of definitiveness when he says, "You grow up speaking one dialect and reading and writing another." And of course that is at the heart of the problem, and that is part of the reason why this country breeds "perhaps a poetic people." In writers as different as William Gass and Eli Mandel, in writers as close and as far apart as Meridel

Le Sueur and Carol Shields and Carol Bly, we see the eruption of words into the gap between the two dialects that contain and open up our lives.

But I was going to tell you a story, and perhaps I am telling you a story. Between the years when Wallace Stegner was a child on the Frenchman River and the time when he published his book, I as a child paid a visit to what at the time we called the Whitemud River. But come to think of it, that's what Stegner resolved to call it.

My visit took place during my first time on the prairies, before I went away and read *Wolf Willow* and came back. The chronology of a story is either difficult or a lie, I find.

I grew up 200 miles north of the American border, in what is called Central Alberta. The town of Eastend sits on the banks of the Whitemud, just a few miles north of the line. I had an aunt, Aunt Maggie, in nearby Shaunavon; she was married to a homesteader from St. Paul who hadn't laid eyes on a farm until he found himself farming. My father had homesteaded for two years just north of Shaunavon, before homesickness drove him to join most of his Ontario family where it was homesteading in Alberta. He had friends in East-end.

In 1936 my father bought a new green four-door Ford. I remember vividly because when we went to pick up the car I was teased about the car dealer's daughter,

Belva Jacobs, and as a result I fiddled with the handle of the door on the drive home and accidentally opened the door and accidentally fell out of the car. An early experience of falling in love and one that continues to inform my prairie life.

But I was going to tell you a story.

My father, having bought the car, revealed he had bought it because we were about to embark on what could only be described as an epic journey—to visit relatives and friends in southern Saskatchewan.

I remember our first encounter with abandoned farms. Our first look at dried-out country. I remember my father stopping the car in what seemed the open middle of nowhere; he and my mother and we three kids got out of the car to stare in disbelief at the bare fields that should have been fields of wheat. I remember the hammer and blur of grasshoppers on the flat windshield. I remember our first encounter with playmates who stopped playing and ran behind a granary to vomit, because of what they were or weren't eating.

I was nine years old. When we got to Eastend, I was convinced we had come to the end of something; to this day the name Eastend fills me with images of falling off the edge of the world. That, too, is in the nature of love.

We were visiting people who lived in a house near the Whitemud River. It was in that house I first heard about the cow in the quicksand.

For much of a lifetime now, two narrative possibilities—two speech acts—have quarreled in my mind.

Part of me is persuaded that I actually saw the cow in the quicksand. That part of me is still horrified at the sight of the cow, its head and the thin line of its backbone showing in the quicksand, the terrified cow snorting, frothing at the mouth, the helpless men trying to get a lariat onto the cow's head without themselves getting stuck, then succeeding, then discovering that by tying the lariat to the bumper of a car high up on the riverbank they would only succeed in dismembering or even beheading the cow.

There is another part of me that suggests I never actually saw the cow. That part of me suggests that I and the other kids were told the story to keep us from playing along the riverbanks and down in the drying quicksand and risking our lives.

In that version the horror is of a different and possibly more ominous nature.

We were told the quicksand had no bottom. We have on the prairies various notions of bottomless, some of them having to do with going to hell. I remember that Battle Lake was said to have no bottom, and when one of my uncles took me fishing there, I sat motionless in the middle of the old rowboat, not yet knowing I was by accident to acquire a surplus of deaths. When one of the Messner boys dived into Dried Meat Lake and didn't surface, ever, people said it was no wonder the searchers couldn't find young Glen, he had dived in a place where the lake had no bottom.

I liked those stories. They became part of a novel I wrote years ago, *The Words of My Roaring*. But the business with the quicksand was different—still is different. When I began to realize that of all the stories that surround us, only a few take hold of our minds and shape our lives— by the time I got to that realization, it was too late to decide between the two versions of what had happened.

My only justification for making a private difficulty public is a hard-earned suspicion that here on the plains/prairies, just as we often talk between two dialects, so must we often talk between two versions of the story. It is no accident that Wallace Stegner, the writer who rode away in order to write, returning to the town he calls Whitemud, encounters most painfully, most tellingly, the writer figure, Corky Jones—the double who did not leave at all, who could never leave.

I return to Dennis Cooley and his poem for and about his father and the quotation from Hank Snow:

Just to think it could be
Time has opened the door
And at last I am free
I don't hurt anymore

But, theory and hope alike be damned, the fact remains, the cow is in the quicksand.

Surely one of the intentions of literature is just this: to acquaint us with the dangers of and to coax us into intimacies with the landscapes we wear. I remember a tailor in England who was fitting me for a suit; he checked my fly and asked in a voice at once elegant and discreet, "Sir, do you dress to the left or to the right?"— a question that to this day makes me slip unobtrusively into men's stores, or women's stores for that matter, and hesitate insanely in front of full-length mirrors.

"You grow up speaking one dialect and reading and writing another." Stegner's book locates his dictum in storytelling itself. We feel the gap between the stories we know in our pores—the stories we feel in the daily weather of our lives—and the stories we are officially taught.

But how do the plains enable us to recognize ourselves as writers, then enable us to write? Stegner insinuates an explanation:

> *. . . I have not forgotten the licking I got when, aged about six, I was caught playing with my father's loaded .30-.30 that hung above the mantel just under the Rosa Bonheur painting of three white horses in a storm. After that licking I lay out behind the chopping block all one afternoon watching my big dark father as he worked at one thing and another, and all the time I lay there I kept aiming an empty cartridge case at him and dreaming murder.*

That dream of murder—that possibly impotent dream of murder—Stegner tells us in the next paragraph, remembering vividly, has faded. "My mother too," he goes on, "who saved me from him so many times, and once missed saving me when he clouted me with a chunk of stove wood and knocked me over the wood box and broke my collarbone: she too has faded." Except that the book bears a dedication: "This is in memory of my mother."

Stegner would escape the flipped coin that won't declare itself by claiming the death of history, the survival, however ambiguously, of memory. But, having declared that allegiance, he plunders historical documents for the making of much of his book.

Resisting history, we take on the burden of a concealed history. Claiming to remember, we discover the slippage that transforms memory into history and fiction alike.

I've announced in my title that the cow gets out of the quicksand. I'm sweating. Remembering Dennis Cooley's poem and its reference in parentheses to "the startling white softness of your body," I'm reminded of my own father.

My father's skin, from his sunburnt neck down, was almost grotesquely the skin of a boy, even when he was my present age. That was because he, a farmer and a rancher for fifty years, never once when out of doors took off his shirt or so much as rolled up his shirt sleeves. He had that kind of abiding respect for the prairie sun.

I offer this curious detail as evidence of his careful relationship to the truths of the world he lived in. He ran cattle in the valley of the Battle River; he grew wheat and oats and barley on the flat land above the valley. And, yes, he told stories.

He was a considerable storyteller. But he claimed no interest in fiction, he trusted rather to the accuracies of his own memory. And that was the power he had over us. I always meant to ask him about the cow in the quicksand, and I dearly regret now that I didn't. But my not asking was the only power I had. It was the only way I had of aiming the cartridge case.

And if the story of the cow was told to us kids— was used against us, one might say—not to elaborate our sense of the world, not to give us a sense of freedom and responsibility, but rather to manipulate us— then we had a right and even an obligation to appropriate the story, with all its errors of intention and detail, and make an effort to tell what was not told.

The margin speaks its one small chance against the design of the center, and on that speaking everything turns.

It was getting on in the afternoon when the adults told us the story; they wanted to be rid of minding kids and get on with having a beer.

In *Wolf Willow* Stegner allows:

As the prairie taught me identity by exposing me, the river val-

83

ley taught me about safety. In a jumpy and insecure childhood where all masculine elements are painful or dangerous, sanctuary matters. That sunken bottom sheltered from the total sky and the untrammeled wind was my hibernating ground, my place of snugness, and in a country often blistered and crisped, green became the color of safety. When I feel the need to return to the womb, this is still the place toward which my well-conditioned unconscious turns like an old horse heading for the barn.

There were four or five boys, two or three girls, in our group. We were a gang, and I suppose hard to manage. Families were bigger those days. My oldest sister, briefly younger than I, was not with us; she has a ferocious memory for detail and tends to blister every account I give of our childhood. Pat would not go with us; she was on the side of history and law even then. But the rest of us, warned about the cow, dodged around behind the house, past my dad's new Ford, and headed straight for the river.

And sure enough, would you believe it: there was a cow in the quicksand.

We kids had to work fast. We had to wrestle and drag two or three huge planks that we weren't quite big enough to carry; we had to scare up a lariat; we had to find a shovel.

Stegner is right. How explain the unconscious, out on the bald prairie? Where do you find the womb?

Sharon Butala tells that terrifying story about young Andrew cutting the dead calf out of the cow.

We kids went through the wolf willow, down over the clay banks where mud swallows nested, onto the treacherous sand. Out of the wind, down there, the smell of dead fish and dead animals was sweet and somehow inviting on the air. We laid two planks end to end, there at the edge of the drying river that was more slough than river that summer day.

We called the cow Bossy. We didn't know her name, but we talked to her, somehow. We talked to the cow. That calmed her down. Then we felt calmer, too; we got the lariat onto her neck. We didn't want to strangle the cow, pulling. One of the boys tried to make a halter, but he didn't quite know how. One of the girls said we should get a rope onto the cow's front legs. We knelt on a plank and dug with the shovel and our bare hands and got the cow's right foreleg free enough so someone could, at great personal risk, reach down and get the lariat around the upper part of the leg.

I've done research on quicksand; it's the shape of the grain of sand that causes all the trouble; the grains are round, like ball bearings; instead of packing down they give way, yield to a weight placed upon them. On top of all that, when you pull up you create a kind of vacuum under the object you're trying to free from the sand.

We pulled and hoisted for a long time before Bossy

came free. But all of a sudden, just like that, she was up to where she could help us, she had her front legs on the plank we were trying to slide beneath her.

She was a three-titter, that cow. This may seem a strange detail, but to us kids, who had grown up on the prairies, it said something. A lot of milk cows, those days, got at least one tit frozen or caught in barbed wire. We never said teat those days, we said tit; teat was a word I learned years later, from an embarrassed teacher; again, a problem in naming and in the relation of education to this our earth, and these the pores of our bodies. That cow had suffered enough, it didn't need any more suffering.

We realized, we kids, we had the detail that would cinch our story. We had won. We had *matched* the adults. When we went up out of the valley of the Whitemud and back to where the adults were having their beer, and when we told them there really was a cow in the quicksand, you know, and you must know which one— that good milker, the three-titter—then they would have to believe our story.

They would have to regret they lied to us in the first place.

Playing Dead in Rudy Wiebe's *Playing Dead:* A Reader's Marginalia

Let me begin with wine.

Wine, in that too-brief moment while it is held in a glass in the hand, both establishes and inverts notions of center and circumference. The very act of drinking a glass of wine is at once a centering and an upsetting.

It is this necessary upsetting of the paradigm that I am, here, now, and marginally, speculating upon, perhaps engaged in. And I begin by recognizing that in order to upset we have to set.

In English studies, during the mid decades of this century, we were much influenced by a critical approach that called itself New Criticism. That approach, we now like to say, spatialized time. Much attracted to binaries, it accomplished a good deal by way of recognizing the models that organize perception and thought. However, it made those models architectural. The binary became a diagram of completion rather than a narrative of its own continuing transformations.

How then do we, once again, embed the model in the narrative of its own uncertainties?

Wine, of course, in its own long narrative, is a legendary embedder.

Wine carries with it, always, a trace of its own past. Yet wine is a premonition. "1990," we say paradoxically in 1992, "will be a good year."

We use wine to narrate rivers, the weather, the fractures in rock. And yet those fractures, that weather, those rivers, narrate the wine. Wine is a shape changer. That ancient city Trier speaks its sunlit history in bottles and caves. One of my great-grandmothers was born in that city, famous as the birthplace of Karl Marx.

Last May, in the city of Trier, surrounded by vineyards, Meeka Walsh and Robert Enright and I were dinner guests in the home of Professor and Mrs. Zirker.

Glasses of wine sit at the margin of one's reach— or at least at the margin of one's socially prescribed reach. Wine, unlike bread or salt, for instance, resides outside the potential of the boarding house reach.

And yet, while bread and salt would seem to be necessities and therefore central, we are often told in a kind of narrative conundrum, "Don't eat too much bread, you'll spoil your appetite."

In my childhood, that was one of the examples of logic that led me to wonder about adults. That wonder—or wondering—persists to this day. To this day I cannot decide whether the child or the adult is at the margin.

But we were about to have a glass of wine, and that is supposedly a marker that defines adulthood, at least according to the laws of Canada. We were in the home of Professor and Mrs. Zirker. While I was not yet impatient to have a drink, I was more than willing to do so.

The serving of wines has a narrative structure, and, as in any narrative, the problem of where to begin is problematic. Or should I say *when* to begin is problematic. The fiction of origin relates centrally to the fiction of center. Narrative, through its curious (and sometimes appalling) dependence on that fiction of a beginning—I invite you to think of Virgil's long deliberations and even narratives on the subject—how does one leave Greece and establish Rome?—becomes a strategy by which one writes the page both full and blank.

To be honest, I was desperate to have a drink. One internalizes the dominant conventions and becomes their slave. But surely Professor Zirker is nothing if not a perceptive host. He served us a *1966 Riesling*—in place of a sherry, he explained.

By that aside, by that marginal comment, he at once located a center and placed himself in a margin that was in some way to be preferred to the center. He is, obviously, a Winnipeger.

The paradigm of center and margin implies a hierarchy. Professor Zirker, who is obviously more of a postmodernist than he might publicly acknowledge, had shrewdly upset the apple cart. Where then was the master narrative and what had begun its interrogation, its subversion?

There are, of course, ceremonies of speech to be gotten through, before one is encouraged to take so much as a sip. Sometimes the reading of the label comes first. Like new lovers both intent on the same praxis, we are stalled by a failure to speak the unlocking word, to make the unlocking gesture. There occurs a kind of perverse or even martyrish prolongation of the delay. Perhaps the erotic is the only paradigm, and that paradigm is ever smudged into unreadability.

I need hardly say that the *Riesling—Mosel Saar und Ruwer, Schweicher Herrnberg, 1966*—was so good that Robert Enright excused himself from the room and went at once into the next room and phoned CBC.

The narrative of Professor Zirker's taste in wines is itself a narrative that has its heroes and its heroic encounters. Serious wine drinkers like David Arnason tell tales of flying across the Atlantic, catching a train, almost missing a connection in Koblenz, stepping off another train in Trier, and then embarking on an exquisite trial by wine tasting that lasted for fifty-two hours and twenty minutes. Dennis Cooley confesses that for one evening of his three-month stay in Germany, for one whole evening, while drinking wine, he did not once cry out, *Zwei Bier.*

But we were talking about center and margin and the beautiful, dangerous dance that constitutes the sometimes frugal, sometimes extravagant economy of their exchange.

To write in the margin of a text is to write by hand; we sign what we say.

When I was a child on these prairies I could not imagine that fruit grew on trees or vines. Fruit in general came from the Okanagan Valley in exquisite wooden boxes, boxes that one could use to play with, to build with, to store books in. My first library was a box that had contained pears.

Grapes, especially, came in wooden baskets shaped of delicately thin, unpainted, sweet-smelling wood, each basket with a handle that curved protectively, erotically, over a cargo of musky blue sweet-smelling grapes, those grapes at times concealed and revealed by the thinnest blue netting. Indeed, my own perverse and at times decentered sexuality may owe a great deal to the ways in which grapes were packaged and distributed in my youth.

At the time, however, I hardly knew or recognized

the connection between grapes and wine. When margin and center lose that connection, when that loving and hating gaze falters, then we have, instead of energy, chaos and entropy. O Canada, oh Canada.

I was saved from entropy by a maiden aunt who picked chokecherries in order to make chokecherry wine. My old aunt was, as people so delicately and correctly put it back then, not all there. She was marginal.

My Aunt Annie and I sometimes picked berries together. Together, we washed them. She hung those ripe, astringent berries in a discarded pillowcase over a large crock. Those chokecherries pressed themselves, filling the air sweet and red. My Aunt Annie was completely at ease—at home—with the idea of time passing. After what seemed to me the very stretch of time we filled the random, empty bottles she had for a whole year been carefully stashing away; into those filled, mismatched bottles we inserted, laughing together, failing and succeeding, corks.

Real wine, in my childhood—bought wine—made its appearance in gallon jugs. It was usually sweet. It bore little resemblance to grapes. My father kept a one-gallon jug in the pantry of our house and a one-gallon jug in the loft of our barn. Both jugs bore the same label; it was a problem in distribution rather than in discrimination. And yet the question of center and circumference was never far away.

In the house you were restricted to drinking only at

certain hours, only on certain days. Drinking, there, was a sign of leisure and class. The womenfolk said they shouldn't. But did.

In the house you drank from your own glass; in the barn you shared a communal glass, each drinker taking his turn—and I use "his" deliberately here, because that escape from the effeteness of the house was a part of gender construction.

The wine in the barn, unlike the same wine in the house, was expected to have kick. Kick, I have since learned, is not generally thought of as a key word in the vintner's lexicon. Professor Zirker, for instance, did not assure us that the delicate and precious Riesling that he offered as a "starter" would have kick. He used other words. Erotic words that had to do with leg and nose. Kick was unambiguously a word from the margin and for the margin. When you knocked back your glass of wine in the barn you made a face, and then you made a noise that was free of the usual signifying phonemes.

I was being taught something about the limits of language. I was being taught something about the dangers and the pleasures of the margin.

One time I was driving around in Alberta with Rudy Wiebe and happened to notice a refrigerator truck parked outside a small prairie town and on it a sign: B.C. FRUIT. I commented to Rudy. He responded by saying he had seen similar trucks parked outside the town of Inuvik, on the eastern edge of the Mackenzie River delta and only a few kilometers from the Beaufort Sea. Up there in the North, where there were no trees, let alone fruit trees, somewhere a young Inuit is growing up persuaded that peaches and cherries, being the erotic wonders that they are, grow in cardboard boxes in the backs of refrigerator trucks. And still we wonder at the perversities of the Canadian imagination.

By the way, one night in Grande Cache, Alberta, Rudy and I were having pizza for dinner and I ordered a half carafe of a cheap Italian red wine. Rudy, who does not drink, tasted my red wine, then said he prefers white.

Bafflement, all my life, has been one of my versions of marginalia.

There in the home of the Zirkers we had arrived at the main course. I cannot now, it embarrasses me to say, remember the main course. But I do remember a side dish.

It was the season of white asparagus. I blush to confess that I had all my life, until that evening, imagined asparagus to be green. For an aging male writer from the Canadian prairies with just the slightest trace of homophobia, cutting up and eating asparagus of any sort calls for delicacy, aplomb, surprise (feigned or real), resolve.

The wine we had with the main course was a *Ries-*

ling Spätlese—Mosel, Saar und Ruwer, Weinbau seit 1650 in der Familie, 1982er Longuicher Herrenberg. Name as paradigm and narrative. The wine was so good that Robert Enright once again excused himself from the table and from the room and went into another room and phoned CBC.

In my childhood, watching the arrival of boxes of fruit and baskets of grapes, I came to realize there was a place somewhere else that was just as potent as my own immediate place in the creation of self and world. We long to know the Other. Desire narrates the limits of attainability.

It seems to me now that we who live in this landscape are not once but twice marginalized. To care for this landscape is indeed to be in love—and love is a state of knowing everything and knowing nothing.

I speak as a writer, but, if pressed, I would extend my notion of the predicament to include Western Canadians in general. We are marginalized by the unspeakably full page of our knowing. History. Literature. America. Britain. Europe. The page announces itself as jam-packed, unalterably full; that is one of the strategies of the full page.

But we who are twice marginalized cannot forget, dare not forget, the unspeakably empty page. The page that is our weather, our rivers, our rocks.

My mind—my tongue—hesitates between the words

empty and blank. I think of those blank pages in Sterne's *Tristram Shandy*. We do not call them empty. I remember the books of my childhood that did not ever mention the prairie world I lived in. Full of words, those pages were blank.

Perhaps the generative moment of my young writer's life came when I realized I had not two *pages* to write upon but rather two *margins* to write in. I could write alongside, with and against, the blackly printed page of our inheritance. I could write alongside, with and against, the unspeakable white glare of what I call, metonymically, North. I have no recollection of when that realization occurred. And, of course, I resisted making a choice.

One summer night, flying back late to Winnipeg from Toronto from a reading, exhausted, I fell into a deep sleep. I was awakened by a gentle poke in the ribs; I awoke to find myself asleep on the motherly shoulder—almost under the arm, against the bosom—of the very large and wonderfully dressed and perfumed East Indian woman who sat next to me; we had begun the descent, she whispered, as to a child. I had the window seat; embarrassed, I turned to the window.

The plane, too, was turning. Far below us, Lake Manitoba was a huge, blank, silver mirror under the eerie subarctic light that tinges the summer nights in Manitoba.

I don't know why I'm telling you this.

Rudy Wiebe, in his book *Playing Dead: A Contemplation Concerning the Arctic* is concerned both with empires and with small gestures of the mind and the body.

Playing dead is a strategy by which one might, hopefully, escape a surprise encounter with a bear. It is, then, a narrative strategy. Playing dead, at best or at worst, is a gesture that must involve both mind and body. Rudy, at one point in his book, says he is not very good at playing dead; that statement is probably the best example of playing dead in the book.

And yet the book might have played dead on Rudy. Published in 1990, *Playing Dead* must have, at the time, seemed marginal to Wiebe the novelist. At the moment, it seems his most telling text.

Playing Dead is a collection of essays first presented as lectures at the University of Toronto. They announce, in book form, an uneasy relationship between speech and writing. Wiebe, in the printed text, says, ". . . this oral storytelling, so refined and perfected by millennia of practice, is the very affirmation of [the speakers'] non-aloneness: the storyteller and the poet/singer presuppose a community of listeners, otherwise nothing can be told."

The subtitle of Wiebe's book, *A Contemplation Concerning the Arctic*, locates the speaker/writer in a field so vast that dislocation and dispersal seem inevitable. That he presented his lectures to an audience that is or pretends to be or denies being at the cultural and political center of Canada further dislocates teller, tale, and audience. Appropriation and subversion were dual participants in Wiebe's elaborate speech act.

The Arctic for Wiebe announces marginality on a grand scale; that is, the margin, by its sheer magnitude, might overwhelm the center.

The explorers who went to the Arctic from Europe were not looking for the Arctic at all. They were not looking for land. They sought instead a passage—the fabled Northwest Passage—a passage by sea from Europe to the Indies—and this in spite of the fact that the river explorers like Samuel Hearne and Alexander Mackenzie had mapped a huge landmass that would seem to separate northern Europe from the Indies. The sailors set out nevertheless—obeying a narrative that said Britannia ruled the waves. What those sailors intended to find was a land of silk and spices. What they found was an obstruction, a full emptiness, an unknown which baffled their very narrative of exploration/exploitation. The center vanished into the margin.

Inside the cover of Rudy's book is a map of the Canadian North with south at the top of the page. We, as trained readers of maps and narratives, are discombobulated. The inversion immediately subverts our assumptions about the picturing of the world. We, as readers, are tipped—upset—into the margin of Wiebe's book.

On the page following the Table of Contents, Wiebe reproduces in black and white a painting made by Robert Hood, a member of Franklin's first polar expedition, shortly before his death in October 1821. The painting is of a Copper Indian guide with his daughter, Green Stockings.

That painting subverts—indeed, almost marginalizes—the stories that are to follow. While the essays concentrate on narratives of the white entry into the Arctic, the reproduced painting points to the irony that makes a Copper Indian the guide to the explorers' discovery of the Copper Indian. A man who lives in the area takes the white explorers to the area they are intent upon describing as undiscovered.

The guide's daughter, Green Stockings, seated at his feet, holds on her lap a snowshoe. She had become the object of a violent love quarrel between Hood and another member of the expedition, Lieutenant George Back. They were only prevented from fighting a duel by an ordinary seaman who "overheard them and drew the charges of the pistols at night."

Green Stockings is pictured as intense, alert, defiant, wearing trousers, and able to repair a snowshoe. At the same time her father, stoical, motionless, standing over her in profile and wrapped in an ankle-length cloak, is nothing if not pregnant.

The European artist/explorer had entered into versions of narrative—and versions of doubt—that threatened one of the tenets of the center–margin paradigm; at least gender must be based on nature, not on construction. The center recognizing itself as dependent male.

Robert Hood, come to margins he had never guessed, was, in all probability, fed the flesh of a dead companion before he himself, on the verge of death, was shot in the back of the head—so that the expedition of discovery might proceed. The center as cannibal.

The three essays are preceded by a section called "The Origin of Ice" in which Wiebe quotes an Inuit legend that begins, "It is said that once, long ago, the earth was warm. No clouds, no snow, no ice or fog existed." In the legend a bear catches Upaum and takes him to her den. "I'm tired from all this hunting," the bear tells her cubs, "and I need some rest, so you watch while I sleep and when I wake up I'll make you lunch."

Quote again: "Upaum lay where she had dropped him, eyes closed, pretending to be dead."

By the end of the story, Upaum has outwitted the bear and in the process created the Coppermine River and snow and ice and fog.

To play dead is to play a trick. It is, at least by the morality of the center, to lie—to tell a lie. Out of that trickery and lying the world is created. Some of us are determined to stick to the margin, come hell or high water.

The first essay, "Exercising Reflection," is a reading of the three expeditions led by Sir John Franklin in his effort to find the Northwest Passage. Franklin and his two ships disappeared in 1846—having in fact, though unknown to Franklin, discovered the best navigable Northwest Passage—only to become immobilized in ice.

Franklin, the agent of empire and truth and the narrative of both, in his immense conviction that the truth is clear and knowable to the man at the center, had failed apparently to read the names on the prows of his two ships. The *Terror*. And, our English reading of a Greek name for the underworld, *Erebus*.

In his second essay, "On Being Motionless," Wiebe considers again, as he has repeatedly in his career, the figure of Albert Johnson—the Mackenzie River delta trapper who played dead by not ever revealing his name or his past or his intentions. Playing dead is a strategy for staying alive, yes. But to play dead is to run the risk of becoming dead.

While Franklin is the figure of authority gone into the Arctic, Albert Johnson is the figure who arrives without authority. He simply appeared. He might have been a fugitive. His name might have been Albert Johnson. He seems to have disturbed the traplines of others; he was reported to the Mounted Police.

Albert Johnson chose silence as his way of playing

dead. He would act, and violently—to the point of killing authority—but he would say nothing. He was hunted down by a loud combination of police and Indians and dog teams and bush planes. In the violence of his death, the silent man became story. He became the words he would not speak, the story he would not tell. Most of us who know the fictitious name of Albert Johnson would be hard put to name the police officer he killed or the Indian from Old Crow who presumably fired the shot that killed the killer. Where is the center? Where the margin?

Another figure who plays dead is the shaman. Wiebe announces his third essay with a fragment from a remarkable Inuit poem, Higilaq's "Dance Song," recorded in 1900.

Wishing to begin to walk,
Wishing to begin to walk,
Wishing to begin to walk,
To Kuluksuk I began to walk.

Higilaq in 1900, with that song, told us all to be poets. We construct ourselves by constructing ourselves. Higilaq doesn't tell us whether or not he made it. The important thing was his translating desire into motion, into process. Into an interplay of language and body.

Franklin walked with the intention of returning to

the center. Johnson walked with the intention of leaving it farther and farther behind. Higilaq, in his walking, dissolves the choice; he concentrates on beginnings, not endings. He seems not to have heard of the center. Perhaps the concern with center is really a concern with ends—perhaps it is always a concern with death.

Wiebe's third essay, "In Your Own Head," honors the Inuit shaman, Uvavnuk. She is seen not as an agent of transcendence or control but rather as a presence in the world:

> *The great sea stirs me*
> *The great sea sets me adrift,*
> *It sways me like the weed*
> *On a river stone.*
>
> *The sky's height stirs me.*
> *The strong wind blows through my mind.*
> *It carries me with it*
> *So I shake with joy.*

Wiebe, in combining an interest in the oral tradition with his own questioning of the phallocentric vision of things, gives himself over to the words of the woman shaman. He delights in the account of how she came to be a shaman:

> *Uvavnuk had gone outside the hut one winter evening to make*

water. It was a particularly dark evening, as the moon was not visible. Then suddenly a glowing ball of fire appeared in the sky and it came rushing down to earth straight toward her. She could have gotten up and fled, but before she could pull up her breeches, the ball of fire struck her and entered into her. At the same moment she perceived that all within her grew light, and she lost consciousness. But from that moment also she became a great shaman.

The quotation speaks Wiebe's own concern to find new ways to be a storyteller. He desires to be healed into new tellings. He must, to find those new ways, find ways of responding to the Delphic motto, "Know thyself." And to know himself now, he must see himself as archeology become arkeology.

Everywhere in the book is Wiebe's word *secrecy*. Against the nostalgia for knowing, he posits a willingness to acknowledge the withheld, the unknown, the disguised, the lie.

Wiebe confronts the indecipherable text. He understands it as Arctic. He writes his marginalia, and that marginalia tells us of the secret. It does not tell us what the secret is. It tells us of the presence of the secret.

I had the privilege of going with Rudy Wiebe to the place—the site—where the great Cree leader, Big Bear, had his first major vision.

With Big Bear we come to another version of playing dead.

Rudy and I drove to the town of—would you believe—Empress, Alberta. Empress is a small prairie town, a ranching town, on the eastern border of Alberta. Just a few kilometers across the border, the Red Deer River flows into the South Saskatchewan River. Above that junction, on the south side of the valley, is a hill called Bull's Forehead Hill.

The river junction cannot be reached by car, and Rudy and I were driving. We discovered, by accident, that the tracks had been lifted from the railway grade. The grade had been turned into a passable gravel road so that cranes and trucks could drive out to the long, high bridge that crosses the South Saskatchewan. A salvage company was about to begin retrieving the steel and iron from the abandoned bridge.

It was a Saturday and the trucks weren't working. Rudy and I in our U-Drive decided to transgress; we drove out along the railway bed that had become a gravel road. Cactus and tumbleweed and black-eyed susans bloomed on either side of the road. There are no trees on the hills in that country.

We drove through a cut in the coulee hills. Straight ahead of us, one of the longest and highest railway bridges in the west pointed across the river toward Bull's Forehead Hill.

Rudy and I walked out onto the bridge. Below us the South Saskatchewan moved eastward; in a pattern of cottonwoods and willows and sagebrush flats, in a pattern of deadheads and sandbars, it met with the Red Deer River that flowed in from the north and west.

Cattle bawled far below us. We looked down onto the backs of flying crows.

Rudy, pointing along the bridge to the skyline above it, began to tell me about the day when that far hill became a central moment—time and space fusing into one—in the history of the Canadian West.

The Northern Cree were at the zenith of their power, having moved out of the northern forest, having adapted to and developed a horse culture that gave them a secure food supply and the leisure to elaborate their society, their culture.

On that one day in the 1840s—in the decade that was the time of Franklin's great success and failure—a Northern Cree in his teens went up onto Bull's Forehead Hill to fast and to pray and to wait for his vision. He would stand in the sun, slowly turning in order to face the rising and descending sun; he would have nothing to drink unless rain fell on his face; he would pray for the vision that would shape his life. You were to stay there, lying down to sleep at night, rising with the morning sun. You were, if you had the courage, to resist the spirits that came easily. You were then to wait for the great spirits.

The vision that came, finally, to the young man who there, in a ceremonial sense, played dead, was the greatest of all the spirits on those prairies: the spirit that came to him was that of the plains grizzly.

That young Cree returned from Bull's Forehead Hill having earned the name: Big Bear.

From that vision, Big Bear got his medicine bundle. From that vision he received his two major powers: the power to be a great warrior in his youth, a great leader of his people in his maturity; a people who, within thirty-five years of the time of Big Bear's vision, would be forced to trade their greatness for a treaty.

Rudy Wiebe, the novelist who recovered for us at least something of the greatness that was Big Bear, standing there in the middle of that abandoned bridge, his black Stetson shading his face, fell silent. Then he pointed down at the scattering of cattle far below us, in the long reach of the valley.

"They almost look like buffalo," he said. "Don't they?"

My own experience of transformation had nothing to do with a plains grizzly but much to do with a common black bear.

I think I have this right.

I was working up North on the Fort Smith Portage on the Slave River. I had hired out to work as a laborer, but, unfortunately, since I was the only person in camp with a B.A. in English and Philosophy, I was assigned the checker's job. I had to keep track of all items unloaded from barges onto trucks for transport past the Rapids of the Drowned and back onto more barges.

I had to work after supper, when the laborers had finished, in order to keep up with the paperwork. One evening I walked into the tent that had been set up over a 2' x 4' frame. In that wonderful dim light that is unique to the inside of a tent on a late fall evening, I thought at first that I saw myself sitting at my desk.

By the time I realized that a large black bear was consuming a chocolate bar I had left on the desk, it was as surprised as I. The two of us got to the narrow 2' x 4' door at approximately the same time. We revised the doorway, making it large enough for the two of us to pass through, albeit somewhat awkwardly, together. The bear and I, for obscure reasons, both struck out in the same direction. The bear had disappeared into the dark forest before I remembered to stop running and to lie down and to hold still. I think I stumbled, actually.

I had a date that night with a woman from the métis community in the settlement called Fitzgerald. She knew a lot about the forest; in fact she did some trapping. We had been walking for a while along a forest trail when she touched me briefly, there in the starlit dark. She seemed to sniff the night. Then said, sharply, "My God, you smell a lot like a bear."

I stopped dead in my tracks. "Should I go take a shower?" I asked her.

She, too, had stopped. A kind of pity—or resignation—welled into her voice. "No," she said. "That isn't what I meant at all."

I could go on.

But we were having a glass of wine.

We were sitting at the table in the Zirkers' home. The dinner was concluded. It was time, Professor Zirker suggested, for one last drink. He was opening two bottles of wine.

Lonesome Writer Diptych

I   I

When my father was in his
prime and I was a boy of
eight, I decided one morning to take his pocket
watch apart—and to put it
back together again—
without his noticing.

He had left his watch on
the dresser in my parents'
bedroom.

2

2

Time to me was a sound. I could hold it to my ear and count its passing. Yes, time passed. I had learned that. Time past was something else. The hands of a clock were called hands. The face of a clock was called a face.

As a child I memorized the exquisite temptation of silence.

It was a confusing parklands silence. Birds in poplar bluffs on open prairie. Orioles and wild canaries. Bird-busy sloughs, surrounded by willows. Mallards and snipes and red-winged blackbirds. A wide, quiet place, full of the sounds of the sky.

3

3

Why did my mother let me take the watch from the dresser and out onto the veranda on the east side of the house? The sun, of course, was hot, that summer morning, on the veranda. There was a

table on the verandah that
my mother used in spring
to place her house plants
on. Or her seedlings. I sat
at that table to work on
the watch that I was going
to dismantle and reassem-
ble.

4

We lived on a farm 100
miles south and east of
Edmonton, near the Battle
River. Rivers are maps of
Alberta, maps that shift,
change, alter the landscape
itself.

It was the Battle River,
with its deep, post-glacial
valley, carving the land-
scape into form, that
defined our parklands
location. My father was
gone all the way to
Edmonton. It was a full

4

One Sunday morning in a
pasture by the Battle River
some of us kids were
playing rodeo and I got
onto a young bull that
bucked—and then I got
off. I got off abruptly and
violently. Getting off
hurt. It hurt a lot. There
are two varieties of cactus
that grow in the coulee
hills of the Battle River.
Pincushion and prickly
pear. And hardpan is hard.
I thought I might be
dying and said so. Some-
one told me to get up off
my ass and get back onto
the bull. In a rebellious

day's journey, going to Edmonton and returning. I had a whole day in which to work on the watch. But why did I want to take apart and reassemble my father's watch without his knowing?

moment I said I was not going to get back onto the bull, I was going to be a writer.

5

5

I think I expected to find in that watch the future itself.

My hometown makes an appearance in the text of Aritha van Herk's novel *No Fixed Address.* The narrator makes mention of a ball diamond and a cafe, this in a chapter called "Memento Mori." Aritha van Herk and I grew up on opposite sides of the Battle River. I had departed before she arrived.

And yet we heard each other's voices in the deep coulees, on the alkali flats, on the shores of Dried

Meat Lake. Voices become
their own bodies. Or is
the other way round? I
forget.

6

My mother brought me
milk, oatmeal cookies.
She lured me into the
house for lunch, then, in
her quiet way of pretend-
ing not to see, let me go
back to my task. And tak-
ing the watch apart had
been easy. As the after-
noon wore on, I saw I was
going to have a bit of
trouble putting it back
together again.

6

Fictional characters allow
us to test ourselves—I am
tempted to say, text our-
selves. Arachne, the hero-
ine of *No Fixed Address*, is a
woman of no fixed
address who is compul-
sively at home.

7

I sometimes see myself, as
a writer now, still sitting
at that table on the verandah, still trying to get the
watch back together
before I hear the sound of
a car that I cannot get see,
before the far tower of
dust lifts itself above the
horizon.

7

I spent much of my life
writing novels that I
thought would enable me
to give Alberta the slip.

Create a replica and enter
in.

Skin out.

8

Had my father left his
watch behind on purpose?
Did I catch a glimpse of a
smile on my mother's face
when I asked her if I
could take it from their
bedroom, out onto the
verandah that faced onto
the road, just—as I so
carefully put it—just to
play?

8

Fred Wah writes from the context I think of as noise. He was trained as a jazz musician and in that manifestation learned to shape noise into the music at the heart of thinking. He surprises us with the elegant shapes that inhabit multitudinous and discordant sounds.

9

For all our contemporary skepticism, we cannot resist reading the world as a small allegory of this or that. A river has something to do with time, but what does it have to do with a watch?

9

To our surprise, in the parklands, we discover that even geography is not a certainty on this fickle planet. Riding the bucking bull of plate tectonics, we hang on for dear life to a floating world.

10

It was late in the afternoon of that hot summer day when my father drove into the yard, back from the city, his mysterious purpose—I forget what it was—accomplished. My mother had been listening, too, for the car, watching. She went out

into the yard to meet my
father.

10

Ordinarily I would have
beat her to the car. She
went to the car and spoke
to my father before he
opened the door.

It is not possible to write
an autobiography. By the
time I learned that lesson
it was too late for me to
avoid the necessity.

The poet Doug Barbour,
trying to escape into the
language of absent occa-
sion, turns space into a
road. Monty Reid, that
geographer of the mind's
discontent, maps the
blunt imaginary.

Robert Hilles, in the
graphing of a moment's
enduring pain, finds the
long poem, even the lyric
narrative of dislocated
time.

By borrowing fragments
of other lives I borrow an

autobiography of my
own. I disappear, only to
discover that I have once
again made a turn in the
labyrinth and met the
monster with the body of
a human and the head of
a bull.

Or is it the other way
round? I forget.

11

There was for me, at one
time, literally no way in
which I could imagine
Alberta as the stuff of a
novel. I went to Montreal.
In Montreal I rented a
garret, because I knew
writers were supposed to
live in garrets. I had read
as much somewhere in a
book.

11

My father came up the
steps of the verandah and
looked at the table and at
his watch. I wasn't looking
at him, so I can only guess
now that he looked at his
watch.

12

The promise of mountains. The promise of glaciers. But those promises are without pastoral implication. They announce a fugitive concern. By hiding one insists that one is part of the landscape.

"Too bad," he said. "Too bad about the watch. I was going to give it to you."

12

He had made it home, just in the nick of time, for supper.

Family Reunion Cowboy Poem

1 *(refrain, when required)*

Hello Heisler, we're all here
It's time to serve the sausage and beer

We've come to visit old friends and new
It's time to tell a story or two

2 _____

Back in the days of the party line
Your neighbors knew if your cows were fine

And if you happened to go on a date
The rubbernecks knew if you got home late

3 ———————

Back in the days of Henry and Anna
The only rhyme they could find was banana

A beer was a dime, a banana was less
But Henry chose beer, we have to confess

To this day in Heisler, as you can see
You cannot find a banana tree

4 ———————

From Hastings Coulee to the Spring Lake hall
(Except when the roads were bad in the fall)

From the Wanda church to Round Head Creek
(Except when you stopped to take a leak)

And all the way from Camrose and Strome
a wedding dance would call us home

But this reunion will top them all
As we answer that old family call

ROBERT KROETSCH

5 ———————

Pig knuckles and sauerkraut
Now what the hell is this poem about?

God in heaven and damn fur dumpt
Don't ask me, you've got me stumped

6 ———————

Back in the days of Hilda and Paul
A trip into town was a one-day haul

And the trip back home, we're happy to tell
Began with a stop at the Heisler Hotel

The train arrived three days a week
(Unless they stopped to take a——break)

Binder repairs came in by rail
Henry Hauck put up the mail

Kids went to Charlie's to have a treat
While the men waited across the street

7 _____

We'll tell the truth or spit to die
Hilda made the world's best pie

Rhubarb, raspberry, saskatoon
And any fruit that was ripe in June

But her flapper pie—please have no fear—
Was better than a game of schmier

8 _____

At playing whist Paul gave a test
Pat and Harley were the best

And nowadays Lou does okay
Unless he gives the ace away

But in the days of horse and cutter
One bad play made Paul sputter

9 _____

Hello Heisler, we're all here
It's time to serve the sausage and beer

10 _____

The night of the Galahad New Year's Dance
Was more than a case of ants in your pants

Big Bob Kroetsch was on a blast
You could tell at a glance that he wouldn't last

The wine was served in gallon jugs
The girls had to dance with some silly mugs

The snow was deep and the road was ice
Yet midnight supper was kind of nice

Sister Sheila phoned home to say
Though she hadn't made it she was on her way

Most of the drivers hit the ditch
The whole darn trip was a son of a—gun

11 _____

Kunigunda and Martin followed the sun
In eighteen hundred and forty-one

It wasn't till nineteen eighty-eight
That all their descendants sat down and ate

At that first reunion, by wonderful chance
Kay and Al showed us all how to dance

Now their daughter Kelly is leading the way
With our newest addition—so far today

12 _____

We were driving to Forestburg with Jane at the wheel
She said, this road has a funny feel

You're not on the road, we tried to tell her
Even Jane is a bit of a heller

You're not on the road, you're out on the shoulder
Just mind your own business, she said, you're older

The cops behind her put on their smiles
She drove on the shoulder the whole twelve miles

13 _____

We've come to see old friends and new
It's time to tell a story or two

Heisler is where our friends are at

Home is where you hang your hat

This is friendship, this is love
Thank the bright stars up above

(repeat)

This is friendship, this is love
Now we're really in the groove

D-Day and After: Remembering a Scrapbook I Cannot Find

I want, in a tangential and I hope at the same time central way, to remember a little bit of what our world was like fifty years ago—back then, as we say. Back then, here on our prairies, in the middle of a world war.

I was tempted to call this "Painted Legs," because one of my most vivid memories of the war years is of high school girls and young women dabbing stockings onto their legs. All available silk, we were told, was going into the making of parachutes. The stockings came in a bottle and were applied with a cloth or a sponge. The real test came when a woman had to draw a seam up the back of her leg with an eyebrow pencil.

That kind of detail, and that kind of memory, is what we might—or might not—use in making a scrapbook. In keeping a scrapbook.

I was in junior high and then senior high between 1939 and 1945, and there in a four-room school in a small Alberta town a farsighted teacher started her students on the task of keeping scrapbooks about the war that began one morning in September when the sky was gray with the promise of rain and the farmers like my parents were busy trying to finish harvest before the rains came. I did not at the time know that wars tended to begin after the crops were in and the men who harvested them were free to be called into military service. I was soon to learn. The young men and the not so young men in our community in 1939 were some of them under- or unemployed. Some were bored. Some wanted to escape from a small town. All of them were in quiet ways patriotic. Within a few months after harvest, all of them were gone.

Keeping a scrapbook was a task indeed. A chore. It was made easier by the arrival of fat copies of the *Winnipeg Free Press Weekly Prairie Farmer,* but even that famous newspaper and its headlines offered short stay.

Only years later did I recognize how much the keeping of a scrapbook had taught me about the world and about writing. By then I had lost the scrapbook I kept. And yet it remains for me one of the most instructive books I ever wrote. Or read. And because I cannot find it, I can go on making revisions, additions. It is still in many ways my story of the war.

A scrapbook is an exceptional kind of book in that it comes to us as a collection of blank pages. We must become authors before we can become readers. Or perhaps we must become readers before we can become authors.

Right there is a lesson that first-year students struggle to learn. Perhaps instead of giving each new student a great heap of books to read, we should present each with a blank book and invite him or her to fill it with the story of how one gets an education.

Scrapbooks transformed us into historians, into journalists, into gossips, into storytellers, into autobiographers.

Perhaps no book is better suited than a scrapbook to recording the personal narrative of war—a war with its terrible surprises, its unexpected joys, its possibility or impossibility of conclusion. And certainly for those on the home front during a war, for the women and children who were, in a certain sense, left behind, it offered an opportunity on a personal basis to deal with the vast absence created by war.

That absence was part of what we now, a half-century later, with the gift of hindsight and some guidance from feminist writers, call a patriarchal story—a story in which the woman stays in the castle while the man goes into the forest or out onto the sea—or off to battle.

Those of us who were on the home front lived in a world that was in profound ways matriarchal.

On the most literal level, women played an important part in the arenas of production and service. The poet Phyllis Webb told me how her mother, in Victoria B.C., worked in the Boeing plant that was established there, and at night drove a taxi; all this in the process of raising three children and watching her older son go off to serve in the army.

From my hometown of two hundred people and from its surrounding farms, fifty-five men and three women went into the services. Obviously, women kept the community going. And not simply in a material way. Their spirit and savvy and humor sustained us.

Coffee and meat and sugar were rationed. This at a time when a good part of the summer was spent in canning vegetables and fruit in preparation for winter. A fifty-pound sack of sugar was a treasure, and the women developed a system for finding and sharing sugar that rivaled the men's elaborate system for getting enough rationed gasoline to keep vehicles moving.

Living in that matriarchal world was for me one of the most instructive and sustaining experiences of the war.

It was the women who waited for that worst of all arrivals, a telegram. They lived with the tension and the anxiety of waiting for reports of a death or injury, reports of someone missing in action.

The waiting was based on the model of the love story. A painful separation, in a love story, becomes the cause of speech. It occasions the telling. The loved one, by the absence of the lover, is forced into telling the story of that love.

The scrapbooks we kept during the war were tales of love. That love ranged within the scrapbook from a love of country to the love of a parent or brother or husband. On its darker side it might announce an attraction to violence or even to catastrophe. At its best it gave voice to much that was not spoken by individuals who were expected to sacrifice the particular moments of their individual lives for a greater intention.

A contemporary theorist might argue that the scrapbook was in some way an especially feminine art form—like the short story as practiced by women writers like Alice Munro and Margaret Laurence a decade ago, it allowed for all the interruptions of a busy daily life. It could be worked on for a few minutes now and then, or in the evening after a hectic day. It could, further, reflect the myriad interests and concerns and distractions that made up a woman's daily life. That in contrast—the theorist would say—to a man who was able to give eight uninterrupted hours a day to a particular task.

I don't pretend to have answers. I am much more interested in the questions we ask ourselves than in the answers we hide behind.

As you have guessed, I am trying to talk a scrapbook of those years that now find their focus in June of 1944.

A scrapbook is made up of fragments—or, as its name insists, of scraps. This apparent or real contradiction is enormously important in the making of the scrapbook—and for that matter, in the making of modern art.

Collage has been a major technique in the art of the twentieth century. The great Modernist artists—Picasso is one of many—discovered that by cutting pieces out of newspapers and pasting them into their paintings they could at once reflect their contemporary worlds, explore the arbitrariness and fragmentation of those worlds, and make statements about the possibilities of the future.

In keeping a scrapbook one faces first of all the matter of choice—what scraps to choose when the newspapers and magazines and documents that we look at in a single day would fill an entire scrapbook and more. And then to make matters more difficult there is the question of how one might organize those scraps, once chosen, on something as small as a page in a scrapbook.

By these processes, one either abandons one's own story—or takes charge, takes responsibility, for the shaping of that story.

Our lives are often informed by small moments that come to have a great significance. Chaos theory has it that a butterfly fanning its wings in Borneo might by some elaborate chain of events cause a tornado in Winkler. Now and then a small event shapes the vast and various forces that we call the weather. According to chaos theory, the seeming confusion has a shape; the trouble is, the shape is so complex that we as humans cannot get a handle on that shape—at least not until the tornado has come and gone and left us in the middle of mess and ruin.

The same proportions and disproportions shape the weather of our lives. We have an experience that almost goes unnoticed or unremarked, then we realize years later how that event shaped our being or our fate.

One such shaping event occurred for me at the time of the landing of Canadian soldiers on the beaches of Sicily.

At that time, back in 1943, a radio journalist—I think it was Matthew Halton—reported that the Canadian soldiers after their first hours on the beach and under fire became avid readers of the first newspapers to reach them.

As a boy I was fascinated to learn that a man, there in the midst of battle, would want to read an account of a fight while he was fighting it.

I suppose I should be embarrassed to confess this, I who am now a writer and a teacher of literature. My only defense is that now I am a writer and a teacher because I didn't at the time understand, and I wanted to.

Those soldiers, risking their lives to make the events—and all the army casualties from my hometown were from the Italian campaigns—wanted to know the shape of those events. They wanted someone to make an informing narrative of the confusion. They wanted someone to put the fragments—the scraps—into order.

Those soldiers on that beach, looking for "the story" on a printed page, became for me a part of what it is that makes us enter university and study the arts and the sciences.

We must set out to get an education, and at the same time we must learn to resist much of what that education tells us to think or do.

The great stories—the quest stories, the stories of love and war—what we call the master narratives—are instilled in us from an early age on, through books and films and now through television.

It is difficult for us to imagine a world without or preceding TV. But during the war we at home listened compulsively to the radio. One would try to be at home at certain hours to "listen to the war news." The radio, along with newspapers, made an explanatory narrative of the chaos that surrounded our individual lives.

The scrapbook made room for the individual inside or even in resistance to the larger story. It made for humor at times. It left us a space to write our own headlines—sometimes in crayon, because the paper was too cheap to take ink.

Scraps allowed us to participate in the story without being swallowed into invisibility.

As children we collected scrap for the war effort.

Cigarette packages contained silver foil, and smokers those days discarded their empty packages wherever they happened to be when the package was emptied. We as kids went around and stripped out the foil and wrapped it into a ball which we then took to school for shipment to collection centers.

We gathered bones, out on the prairies. The bones were to be used to make fertilizer and gunpowder. We hauled them into town to sell to dealers, and as a dealer told me years after the war, a good dealer never overestimated the weight of a load of bones when making an offer.

We gathered scrap iron for sale to the local blacksmith, who sold the scrap iron to dealers who filled boxcars with the discarded machinery from prairie farms.

We gather scraps together to make a scrapbook, and in the process we explore one of the ways in which we make meaning in the twentieth century. We keep a scrapbook. Then we ask: How does one read a scrapbook?

We must learn to read the gaps, the silences, the long story behind the snapshot that captures a split second of time and fixes it in a small and unmoving frame.

A scrapbook is almost pathetically made up of scraps. Yet the idea of scrap implies a larger whole, an organized universe, an explanatory mythology, from which the scrap was taken or has fallen away. Or it might harbor that implication.

That doubt has informed a good deal of my notion of what writing is. What if the scraps are the story? Our lives on the prairies often went unrecorded; they survived as a collection of photographs in a shoe box, a scattering of stories told around a kitchen table. They survived as a scrapbook. But was there something else that was more unified, more complete?

Margaret Laurence, in her account of Manawaka's "nuisance grounds" in her novel *The Diviners*, suggests that discard and dirt might be as much inventions as is any vision of completeness. And Margaret Laurence is our great storyteller of the home front during World War II. I only speak here because of her absence.

Love and war are two of the great organizational themes of both literature and life. They came together for me in a small way in my scrapbook.

A two-engined training bomber crashed near our home. The crew of five walked away with a few scratches and bruises, but the plane was such a wreck—such a scrap heap—that we who gathered to stare were left wondering how anyone had survived at all. And some of us in high school were taking air cadet training.

The local paper somehow got permission to print a picture of the crash and included in the story an account of the lives of the young men from England and Australia who were part of the British Commonwealth Air Training Plan and who were in the plane that crashed.

Locally, we knew that the young English pilot had gone fifty miles off course in order to waggle the wings of his plane at a cousin of mine who lived on a farm and whom he had met at a dance.

A scrapbook is made up of stories—and of gaps and silences. A scrapbook is a kind of code; the code allows us to bring into play whole areas of memory. And desire. And laughter.

The role of laughter in difficult times or difficult lives is as central as that of tears. Perhaps I am skipping the role of desire. I remember a great deal of laughter along with all the tension and the waiting.

The young women who painted stockings onto their legs were on their way to dances, and the dance was surely an important place of laughter during the war.

To go back for a moment to the painted-on stockings: a girl I was dating developed an obsessive fear of rain. The slightest splash made a run in her stockings. She and all her friends scurried for cover at the sight of a dark cloud, and on the prairies dark clouds are not hard to find. In my own way I developed a parallel fear of rain, because a date taking cover with all her friends became a communal gossip session rather than a date.

Necking was the fashion those days. I have a suspicion the young now have no idea what that might mean. But to go out and neck in the 1940s represented an epic undertaking. Gasoline was rationed, so one had to decide whether or not to risk getting to a dance by using purple gas—the nonrationed gasoline that was dyed and to be used in agricultural machines only— and the Mounties actually set up check points and tested the gasoline in gas tanks. A car was allowed 120 gallons per year; try necking on that allowance in the middle of winter with the temperature at −30°F and no possibility of turning off the car engine for hour after hour.

Then there was the problem of tires. The tires made of synthetic rubber would blow out in warm weather or freeze stiff in cold weather. On the morning of a cold winter day all four tires would be frozen flat on the bottom side, and would bounce along that way for a considerable distance before thawing out. I remember changing six tires out on deserted country roads in the course of one January, all in a desperate and by and large vain attempt to get to a neighboring town and to go out on a date. And neck.

I must mention one other detail here that has escaped most historians. Men wore suspenders back in those days. As a part of wartime economy, suspenders were made of cloth, with a mere two inches of elastic at the back, just above the buttons. Make the slightest sudden or excessive movement, and you tore the buttons off the back of your pants. And then try jitterbugging.

Liquor rationing became the cause of infinite scheming and the source of much laughter. People who had never had a drink in their lives rushed to get their ration cards the day they were twenty-one. Those with ration cards were allowed one bottle of spirits and one case of beer per month. Talk about scraps. A version of lemon gin seemed to be the only drink that was not sent forward to the troops, presumably because not even the most desperate soldier would drink the stuff. The resultant hangovers were the source of the famous saying, "I was so hung over I was afraid I wouldn't die."

In the spring of 1944 rumor had it that the invasion of the continent was imminent. We lived by rumor; rumor was part of the daily drama of the war. Rumor circulated below the level of news reports and casualty lists and newspaper headlines.

The Japanese were rumored to be floating strange diseases into the country on mysterious balloons. The balloons turned out to be our own weather balloons.

By the spring of 1944 there were almost no baseball players left in our small town. I was invited, at the age of sixteen, to play first base for the Heisler Cardinals. Let me say that in a community where baseball was more of an obsession than was hockey I was not a gifted player; even I, in fleeting moments of self-knowledge, recognized as much. But I was large enough to constitute a considerable target for someone throwing to first.

I was at baseball practice the day we learned of the landings in Normandy. Rumor became reality. The soldiers who had waited so long were in action.

We had met at the ball diamond for practice, we, the young and the old. Someone mentioned fielding practice. But no one walked out into the field. We sat around home plate and talked, trying to guess what was happening to our relatives, our friends, who had waited so long for that fateful morning.

We were sitting there, motionless, and our lives were undergoing radical change. Another kind of hope was announcing itself, on a thin line of beach along the French coast.

We were not there. How then could we be there?
Scraps are left over from the making of a book—

that is, from the making of a cohering narrative, from the establishment of beginning, middle, and end.

Scraps also have the paradoxical ability to become a book.

With scissors and brush and paste, we take the scraps and make a book of our own.

A scrapbook acknowledges its own limits. One cannot put a beach into a scrapbook, at best only pictures and accounts of a beach.

When those thousands of men waded ashore on the beaches of Normandy, or dropped behind the Nazi lines by parachute, they went beyond the limits of our plain stories. In the discourse that followed upon their actions, they became heroes.

When pasting things into a scrapbook you must take care not to leave any grit or grain in the paste; those small grains become lumps as the paste dries. One quickly learned to dip a finger rather than a brush into the paste.

By small acts of caring, we paid tribute. We selected headlines for inclusion. We cut out the casualty lists that our parents so reluctantly studied. We selected stories of torpedoed supply ships and the destruction of U-Boats. We arranged on the blank pages of our thickening scrapbooks the strange array of the hats of war—the white or navy blue flat-topped hats that sailors wore, the wedge-shaped hats that airmen and soldiers wore when posing for pictures to send home, the berets that some of the soldiers wore, the khaki hats with earflaps that they wore in winter. The few officers hats worn by boys who went from small towns to war. The helmets that soldiers and airmen wore in battle. A strange pun, the past tense of wear.

Those hats took on faces—and stillness—against the white of the scrapbook page.

We on the home front sensed there was nothing we had done or would ever do that would compare in significance with what those men were doing, on D-Day and the long days following.

We knew the war in Europe was drawing to a close, but we could not guess exactly when that would be. On the day of the sudden announcement, the small towns on the prairies launched into celebration. There was a great scramble to find orchestras. To celebrate meant to dance, and to dance meant to have live music in the community hall. And there was no rain that night to ruin anyone's painted stockings.

Within a matter of weeks there were, in the bookstores, hastily written histories of World War II. We were eager to read the completed shape of that story, and I bought and read one of those books.

I was in for another of the surprises of war. And I was about to experience another of those accidental moments that echo and enlarge as time goes on.

That history of nearly six years of a world war had

in it one paragraph on Canada. You can no doubt guess what that paragraph was.

It was a very brief account of the Canadian raid on Dieppe.

For six years our Canadian lives had been dominated, shaped, determined by the war, and there in that text all our efforts made no mark whatsoever.

That book, instead of giving me a sense of my story, a sense of my identity, made me feel invisible.

My teenage life had been preoccupied with the war. In a way we of that generation were never quite teenagers. We were something else. We were children becoming adults with no intermediate stage.

Perhaps that, too, is something I am trying to talk about.

The first wave of veterans returned to our lives in the fall of 1945. I went as a first-year student to the University of Alberta along with literally thousands of men and women who were returning from war. And for me they were not the completion of my scrapbook but rather its continuation.

I wanted to go from keeping a scrapbook to writing novels. I was admitted to a course in creative writing taught by the legendary teacher, Dr. Salter—the man who taught writers like W. O. Mitchell and, later, Rudy Wiebe. At the first class we were asked to describe briefly who we were.

One student was a former fighter pilot who mentioned in passing that he could not turn out his light at night. Another had edited a newspaper for the Army in England for three years. A woman had helped organize convoys that set sail from Halifax. When my turn came I said I was fresh out of high school and just finished helping with harvest.

We were heavily under the influence of Hemingway at the time, and believed that to be a writer one had to go out and seek dangerous experiences. I had been nowhere, I felt. I had done nothing, I felt. After class I went and dropped the course and registered in a course called Victorian Poetry.

I should have remembered my scrapbook and its chaotic design and its lessons in how one finds and tells a story. This is not to say I did not like the course in Victorian Poetry. Matthew Arnold had been to Dover Beach and knew the sound of contending armies.

Being in university, and in residence, with veterans, taught me that my scrapbook was going to be slow in its concluding.

I remember the profound humanity of those men— and I say men because back in the 1940s women were never allowed into the hallways of a men's residence.

Those men had been through an experience that might have made them doubt their own humanity, or humanity at large. Instead, they embraced with passion all the possibility—and all the diversity—of their lives.

They studied hard and they played hard. They gambled for sums of money I had not imagined. They drank quantities of whiskey that no ration card had ever allowed for. They listened to varieties of music I had never heard or heard of, they read all kinds of books that were not on the professors' reading lists (some of the veterans had been to Paris). They dared to dream out loud. And they cared for each other and for learning.

They, too, lived with the idea of a scrapbook, those veterans. They had lived what were surely full and dangerous lives. And yet they were, each of them, about to fill up a book that had in it many blank pages.

Homecoming implies a going away. A departure and return. And possibly that is the oldest story—the story of going away, and returning. And returning with some sort of knowledge that changes the way one lives at home.

We began to travel during World War II, and we have not stopped since.

What does travel do to meaning? What does it do to the idea of the scrapbook?

If McLuhan was right when he said that the medium is the message—and in many ways he was right, I suspect—then the scrapbook itself is the message.

The scrapbook becomes a model. A paradigm. It tells us how to organize ourselves. It tells us how to think about what we are.

I have already mentioned the idea of collage, the placing of stories or images side by side in such a way that they suggest a possible meaning without insisting on it. There is also in the scrapbook the notion of the interrupted story, or, more significantly, the digression. The digression often tells us what the main line of narrative cannot accommodate; it tells the reader what is being left out in order to make the story hang together.

And I should mention, by the way, what happened to me and that baseball team. I survived as a member of the team through the summer of 1945. In the summer of 1946 I returned home from university under the illusion that I might, in fact, have underestimated my own abilities as a baseball player.

One evening someone knocked at the door of our house.

It was the team coach. I hoped he was coming to tell me to attend a practice where I might at least try out for first base.

The coach simply said that he needed the uniform I still had in my closet; the team was about to play on the coming Sunday and the new first baseman was just about my size.

Is life at the university the main narrative line or a digression?

I now understand that the keeping of a scrapbook is an important literary act. It is not only an assertion of our place in geography—and my imagination is insistently geographical. It is a model of how one might locate oneself in the stories that explain our being present. Our being here.

Fifty years after the events, we talk together now of a war that our children and their children know only through books and films and photographs. That is one of the unnerving dimensions of teaching—talking to students who think of your own intense experience— back then—as distant history badly recorded.

One of the ways in which we say "we were there" is through our scrapbooks.

I cannot show you the scrapbook that I kept but cannot find and now can only talk about. But just to make it at all was sufficient.

That essential recognizing, that compiling, that imagining, enabled me then to survive—and even to hope.

A scrapbook is a story; a story is about hope.

Sitting Down to Write: Margaret Laurence and the Discourse of Morning

*E*arly morning is the time of the mind's revisioning. In the turn from dream toward daylight it finds the crack in everything of which Leonard Cohen sings. It is the time of disconnection and connection, a dangerous time, a liberating time, as Margaret Laurence shows us in the opening of her novel *The Diviners*. In the third paragraph on the first page, morning having announced itself, we read:

> *Pique had gone away. She must have left during the night. She had left a note on the kitchen table, which also served as Morag's desk, and had stuck the sheet of paper into the typewriter, where Morag was certain to find it.*

We persist in the conviction that the author begins from a blank sheet of paper. This assumption has held among writers and readers at least since the beginning of the Romantic Period. *Tabula rasa. Ab ovo.* Sprung full-grown from the brow of Zeus. Making something out of nothing. The writer as creator. Virgin Mother or Big Bang . . . The very notion bestows upon the author a kind of godhead.

Morag Gunn, sitting down to her typewriter—sitting down to begin—finds she has already begun. Uncannily, the sheet of paper in her typewriter is written upon. The first page of her narrative is written. Morag is presented with characters and an action. In structuralist terms, she is confronted by—and she confronts—a double violation; an unexpected disordering of the world; an unexpected disordering of authorial control.

Morag Gunn, sitting down to begin, finds not only that she has begun. She has been begun. She has been positioned. Contrary to the assumption of authorial freedom, she has been left with almost nowhere to turn. She has been told that if Gord phones, "Tell him I've drowned and gone floating down the river, crowned with algae and dead minnows, like Ophelia."

To begin with, that is not where Pique has gone at all. If Morag delivers the message, she lies. If she does not deliver the message, she fails.

At first glance, then, Morag seems to be caught between lying and failing. She is in between a rock and a hard place. Life—or at least art—has got her, as

149

Christie Logan might say, by the short hairs. Forced to act, she cannot avoid complicity. By that complicity she is empowered. By that same complicity, she is relegated.

Morag Gunn, sitting down to write, finds she has been written to. Intending to send a message, she has received one instead. She is being told what to do by someone who has up and cleared out. If writing is a god-game, then the power appears to reside with the one who is absent, not with the one who is present. But that is the way with gods. Presence announces not the writer's sacred but rather her profane condition. She is in the here and now of time present, place present; she is in a world of contingency, surprise, short-sightedness. Her assignment is not simply to begin; it is to begin from the impossibility of beginning.

"Now please do not get all uptight, Ma," Pique writes, constructing the person to whom she writes. Thanks to Pique, Morag is indeed all uptight. She's wired. She's a wreck. Consider, Pique says, what your writing has done to your Ma-ness. And before you take your Ma-ness too seriously, remember that you are one of Shakespeare's myriad and perishing children.

Morag, by way of response, first off reads Pique's message as writing. She, as much as her daughter, confronts the question of agency. "Slightly derivative," Morag thinks, feebly, bravely, lovingly, of Pique's message.

To announce one's intention to write a novel is to

announce one's intention to write what is already written. We are, as writers, always in the predicament of Goldilocks: "Someone has been sitting in my chair."

The chances of being original are less than slim. They don't exist. It is because they don't exist that one can be original. But that is a Kroetschian argument, not a Laurentian argument.

Morag Gunn sits down at her kitchen table to a typewriter. The kitchen table is one of the marks of her own self-construction—part of what we might call her signature—and the problem of writing what already exists is a problem in signing. Perhaps, then, the kitchen table is not only a mark of Morag Gunn's signature; it is also a mark of Margaret Laurence's signature. But let us avoid that question.

The typewriter signals a technology of writing that offers grave resistance to signatures of any sort. Some of us are old enough to remember a time when one did not write personal letters on a typewriter. To do so would have contradicted one's very intention.

The typewriter signals the Foucauldian technology by which we construct the act of writing—and by which we construct literature. The writer is part of an apparatus that produces the texts that society and culture require in order to be society and culture.

Morag Gunn counters that force—that power—with the kitchen table. With kitchen talk. The busy writer, avoiding work, works by gossiping. She gossips with herself. She brings to bear an alternate technology of production—a feminine technology, one might wish to say—that engages the typewriter in dialogue. She talks around the subject until the talking around becomes the subject.

With her positioning herself at a kitchen table that serves as a desk, she enters into a dialogue with the positioned self created by Pique. By placing her typewriter on that table become desk, Morag at once accepts a technology, and asserts her own agency within the elaborate apparatus that is going to establish her and use her as a writer. She lays claims to gender, to class, to social relationships of her own. But let us avoid those questions.

How does one begin if the page in the typewriter is already written? How does one read that page? How does one write with and against that page? Is it one's own writing that constitutes the intertextuality?

It is the very fullness of the page inserted by someone else in her typewriter that compels Morag Gunn. Tradition has created much of the fullness. But she, too, by the writing of her novels, has done some of the filling. It is the fullness of that page, its overflow, not its emptiness, that enables Morag Gunn to write, even as she is threatened with a silencing.

By sticking that page "into" Morag's typewriter, Pique became the first enabler. In her own devious way, Pique is muse. "Am going west," she writes, the "I" not yet invented for that sentence. "Am going west." "Am" becomes a noun. Almost a proper name. To go west is to find "I" and to lose it in the finding. It is to turn "I" into a continuous exchange of resolving image and fading trace, of disappearance and innuendo and encompassing presence.

Pique's going forward in time carries Morag back into the genealogy of her own writing, and by that process forward, too. Pique's note on the first page of the novel becomes the first page of the novel.

One is able to write one's absence, and in a way that is what Pique does. She writes a one-paragraph novel, and in the process lays claim to all the huge explanatory footnote that her mother will write as a consequence.

But there is another side to the story. The moment of loss invites silence, yes. But it also creates both the site for a speaking and a speaking out. When and where does the pained speaker erupt into words? More to the point—when does the pained body erupt into words? Perhaps it is in the pained body that both Morag and Margaret find signature. But let us avoid that question.

Perhaps there is always another side to the story. The note that Pique sticks into the typewriter positions Morag between two discourses. Morag confronts the contingent and autobiographical moment. Yet Pique, shrewdly, to get to that moment, perhaps to control and shape it, invokes in her own writing the colonializing paradigm implicit in the notion of canonical writing. Perhaps Pique herself has internalized the paradigm. More probably, she reads her mother, that Ma from the West, as someone whose uptightness derives in part from a submission to the inhibiting paradigm that enables a daughter to conclude an abrupt message with the word *Ophelia*.

Morag is caught up elaborately in pedagogy. Pedagogy becomes, obviously, an element in society's technological project. Morag's husband, as an agent of that technology, would diminish and even erase the autobiographical (at least for Morag if not for himself). He would have her embrace the discourses of truth we now associate with modernism and with empire.

Morag, in her resistance to the idea of Artist with a capital A, tries out other discourses. She quickly tells us that she is doing work, hard work, and that she is a tradesperson. ("Don't knock the trade.") And yet from Royland's talk she has learned to venture beyond mere work. From the talk and silence of Christie and Prin she has learned to listen so totally that she is able to risk erasure as well as realization.

Sitting down to her kitchen table and to words, she sits down as an established and experienced writer—but also as a novice, as someone learning again and again, in a postmodern sense, not how to end, but rather how to begin.

Morag Gunn begins her novel by reading. This time she reads a message left in her typewriter, not by past generations, but by the next generation. She positions herself between—among—conflicting discourses. By that positioning she becomes a spokesperson for a Canadian poetics. It is the strategy of a preemptive cultural or political or social or economic force to have one discourse dominate. In Canada, the writer refuses the resolution into dominance. That resistance, that wariness of power, portrays itself in the various discourses at work, and at play, on the first page of Laurence's *The Diviners*.

We as readers, approaching the table, approaching the typewriter on the kitchen table become a desk, approaching the writer at work, discover that the writer at work is not writing at all but rather that she is reading. We as readers reading the text, first of the novel, then of the paragraph in the typewriter in the novel, discover that the first paragraph of the text could not have been the first paragraph of the text because the first paragraph is already there on the sheet of paper in the typewriter in the text, and it was not written by the writer who is writing the novel. Or perhaps it was.

Now we know we are Canadian readers reading a Canadian text about a Canadian poetics of fictional prose. It is, it turns out, necessary, after all, to refer to the description of morning in Margaret Laurence's text. In that description we find the phrase so dear to our students, and now so reassuring to our critic—"apparently impossible contradiction."

And now we are prepared to leap again over the first and second paragraphs, and over the third and fourth paragraphs as well. I see I have said nothing about Pique's having left at night. What is the discourse of night in *The Diviners?* How does that painful discourse engage in equal and balanced and Canadian dialogue the discourse of morning? But let me avoid those questions.

Now we can begin to read the apparently impossible contradictions included in paragraph five: "Pique was eighteen. Only. Not dry behind the ears. Yes, she was, though. If only there hadn't been that other time when Pique took off, that really bad time."

Yes, it is not a difficult text to read. But no, it is though.

She is not here. We miss her. She is here.

Poem For My Dead Sister

I began what turned out to be this poem on the morning when I realized my sister would not live through the day. I could only handle the realization by writing. I was losing it. My sister, on the other hand, was in charge of her own death. Sheila was that kind of person. She was dying of cancer, and she had decided that was the day she would give up the ghost. It was a cold day in late December 1990. We were in Petaluma, California.

Morning

I

in the greenest of comparison, water
reads our trace against corrodibility

ROBERT KROETSCH

sky is a dark virtue, whisk a word
rinse a retrieval off the hard map

klee cries, the verb retaliates,
is isn't not enough to grieve

2

timers hold eggs inside their mouths,
if toast and word of night, a tourniquet

winding awake, the cleavage of resistance,
pretense of dawn, prohibit and to conjugate

release, delusion of both eye and ear,
in jest ingest, the pancake, flowered

3

dribble of today allot, repeated sun
or even if, allow allurement, in

pernicious and rebellion both
a sediment, the sorrow of what is

the fly of destiny, fomenting

158

whine of why, whispered, concatenate

4

the tryst of trust, calumnious
a field of desiccated grass

as is a glod in heaven
not glikely, the rainmaker sled

nor blindman's buff recoup nor
snow hide handkerchief

Before the Leaves

1

the wilted snow obliterate
as obligation feeds exiguous

hurray is ha, is haw
or hem the lucifer of light

leaves will be green, if green
tumescence riddles

2

claptrap of agreenment
whip, disagruntle the fat flake

to tabulate to arid twig
gumboot hollow ditch

the stalwart crow said, caw
the lightest lip of leaf

3

husk and the rind obliterate
frisk first the frosted field

branch, unbrittled, myrtle musk
hope, hope unhoping hope hoped

the bare trees, bare, the
luminosity of eye, itinerary

4

you you, you we, you my
the braked earth, open

open the crocus, cry
soft, the illumined catastrophe

the cratered heart, open, tock
the click of leaves, taking

    Petaluma, CA

   1

tropic having lost itself in posse
jarred in the penumbra

or preternatural permutation
illusory as allusion gifted

carbon insufficiencies surmount
as sun is sun as is

   2

the stenographer of finitude
dark, dark, the whistled woe

winsome, astute, lugubrious
the valley farming solitude

sister and brother better, best
trope the jeered corral

3

then then is the end then
a terrific if, a swizzle

truth and the sleep hold hands, huh
we are all in the same bode

oak tree and the palm alike allay
vining the grape from all astray

4

dreaming a homeward, unaware
find a childhood discompose

the river, fen of fern, hunt
glutted, grained, drought dry

the highway hum, hum ho
ocean, a morning mist, missed

Saying

1

wilderment (be) (ac)cretaceous, else
the mendicant (a dreamer) recollect

(mined full) or heir (the waste) of solitaire
greet gratefully green (or sun as yet unseen)

(across the riding bridge the ridded plain)
sock in the weather and (arouse) the rain

2

as (un)fortuitous as plato's end
re(mark) the toothy bird of (all at once)

sky (and a quit hero) the river's bond
lift aloft (quiescent) pizarro to peru

arrive, arrived (arriven) around arrest
saint of not but silence (and the blest)

3

but bunt, but bound (a dialogue of nix)
root

raise (raucous) the bread truck's element
the pepsi man (accompany, accost) acclaim

(blame is a zero not beheld) the wizard gift
dram is the only measure (thumb a lift)

4

the broker's model bears (the bruin) brunt
(a tournament of stars) flash and the hale

stalk stark (the wrecktitude of wishes)
(fish the dry sand) feint fate

the kitchened apples (and the kindred pie)
sleep in a winter (children learned to play)

Arrangement

1

melothy of mixedness, the crane
chimney the crane, the craw, caw crow

call the caller (not), the guessed gone
livery of wanting, the goshawk, going, gone

the bird is (not), the bird sings, trill, coo
the trail is (not), walking, the toe

2

or boot and booted are (not) one
the rabbit's eye is (not) the gun

the styrofoam is (not) the cup
the leather grip is (not) the glove

the lovers' laugh is (not) a groan
a hunter's sighting is an end

3

beelzebub and flibberjab
one is insect, one is gab

one is mote in moter's aye
one is how to say good-bye

one a will is, one enough
cow and cat at water trough

4

water is as water does
clouding over, sliding down

winter is as water was
wavering the sculpture wind

wind and water weave a tone
wind and winter weave a bone

Visibility

1

sigh the dumb wick burnt
arrowed as of to ever spent

willow and wine a look annealed
flight to the roused nothing, once and was

the truce presented, now a now be were
the track annihilate, choke the bear bare

2

close the reminder, closeted book
choose, the closed book, clapping

clam and gentian reprobate, crotchety
steal at last look, asphodel, remain

sputter, and win and winnowed
rue is rue, unrailed, unravel ravel

3

bust and the lunatic spinner span
travel a stillness, travailed home

the kiss of breaking, teeth, tongue
toddle of losses, laughter laughed

and the holed mouth, mouthing
mouthed, mothermouth unmurmured

4

mesmerized by bane, moon mold
locket of moon, moonlack

but benny diction, loco as loquacious
loco is, cared emily, to interglade

the columbine, a carpet, dread dove
a mover, moved, a baser batter, bold

Figuration

1

the lost life last, we ewe ourselves
she we, astound the crittered riverbed

the wasn't us is all we are and sleep
the harpooned angel, and the crypt accuse

accost the apple and across the bow
home the hunter is, and well the crow

2

fallow the stubbled field, and and, alone
and coulees figurate the crisis wind

and call the dark birds down, the decoys dream
delay, the droning bees deliberate

delay descent, delay, and send the sky
the sky to kiss and elevate the eye

3

and toxic as the hemlock drink of old
the hunter take the cider and the cold

the epigram and eiderdown conclude
brooding and soft, the waders take to air

the willows rime, the far slough clamor call
and wear a noose of ice around its shore

4

delay, descending day, apostrophe
approve the call, the cliff of solitude

appearance peer, onto the glaze of what
is is or muted mood, the naked pot

tip down, and clock unwind the winter tree
and sky and mallard fly the winter free

The Poetics of
Rita Kleinhart

"The question is always a question of trace. What remains of what does not remain?"

I have decided to renounce the writing of poetry and to devote my life during this remaining decade of an appalling century to an examination of the note-books and manuscripts of Rita Kleinhart, the brilliant poet who disappeared on June 26, 1992, at the age of fifty-five. A recluse by nature, she apparently traveled outside Canada only once; she gave only three public readings; she lectured twice to academic audiences. And of course she published the ninety-eight brief poems

(hornbooks, she chose to call them; somewhat preten-
tiously, it seems to me) that are the basis of her quiet
yet enduring reputation.

The unpublished Hornbook #99 may have occa-
sioned, I would like to conjecture, her refusal, for the
final nine years of her life (if we are to believe that she
is dead), to add further to the astonishing series initiat-
ed by poems #1 to #98.

Kleinhart was invited, during the late spring of
1992, to visit Germany and to lecture briefly to the
Canadianists at Trier University. On her way back
from Trier she paid a visit to the Museum of Modern
Art in Frankfurt and while at the museum mailed a
number of postcards to friends. She was not seen alive
thereafter.

Her ranch in Central Alberta—her house overlooking the coulees and the valley of the Battle River—contained at the time of her disappearance neat stacks of
scrawled notes, partially filled notebooks, and, yes,
unfinished (or unfinishable?) poems.

The opening of #99 exists in a number of versions,
with no particular version indicated as her final choice.
On the top of a sheaf of drafts I found two lines on a
single sheet of paper:

I am watching the weather channel.
It is that kind of day.

Rita questioned and even rejected ideas of evolutionary development. She had other fish to fry.

HORNBOOK #84

"Why don't you close doors?" Rita once asked me, when I indiscreetly left a door open behind us. "I was born on a raft," I replied.

I knew how to irk her and at times couldn't resist. Rita Kleinhart was persuaded that her notion of collective biography—the expression is mine, not hers—could not be located in a system of beliefs or a narrative of origins. It could only be located, literally and momentarily, in back doors.

Her fascination with back doors—of houses, of apartments, even of garages and barns and public buildings—announces her interest in collective biography. Her brief but eloquent poems on the subject of the back door speak to and of the pathetic beauty that we create by way of discard and something that one might call denial. Back doors are, she proposes in her notebooks, the escape from transcendence. They are also the escape from so-called good neighbors and possibly from language itself.

I tell you this because my own recollections, along with the neat stacks of paper of which I have made mention, give the lie to the published poems so treasured by Kleinhart's (albeit too few) devoted readers.

HORNBOOK #83

Kleinhart earned the displeasure of some of her neighbors in her generous attempt to write for them a collective biography. Her announced intention of inscribing in her poetry the ninety-nine back doors that were nearest her own led, on more than one occasion, to her being forcibly evicted from so-called private property. Her response was to write on the back of an envelope that was addressed to me but never mailed:

"One cannot, now, be a love poet. Now one can only be a desire poet, or not a poet at all."

Kleinhart sometimes worked from photographs. She would not snap a picture until she saw a person entering into or exiting from the back door in question. The subjects, I hasten to say, survive in those photographs as nothing so much as blurs—surrounded, often, by unintended or even embarrassing detail.

Living in relative isolation as she did, on a fairly large ranch, dear Kleinhart fell prey, along with her isolate desire, to rampage need. Her attempts to *regard* (a verb she much liked) the back doors of near and not-so-near neighbors led to her being labeled not only a recluse, but also a snoop and a thief, a voyeur, a strange bird, and, as some of her farther neighbors put it, a nut case.

Collective biography, of course, attempts to locate collectivity at the bottom, so to speak, not at the top. Rejecting notions of the religious or political transcendental or the Platonic ideal or, apparently, the very narrative of love, collective biography, Kleinhart somewhere in her heaps of notes remarks, is a notion that must of necessity be full of shit. Now and then she blundered into a truth. But surely her idea owes its origin to a deviant reading of Bakhtin, a man she pretended never to have heard of.

Somewhat fascinated by prairie cemeteries, she was ever attracted to the bare wooden crosses she found in those small rectangles of fenced sod. She worshiped, in her own way, the peeling white paint, the smell of rotting wood, the worn pathways of ants—and at the same time she loathed anything those crosses might, as the expression has it, signify. It was the stolid, dumb, wooden repetition, from graveyard to graveyard, that fascinated her.

She found that same stolid, dumb, fascinating repetition in back doors.

Back doors are the very locus of discharge and communality. Kleinhart mentions at least three times in her notes a particular occasion when, injured at play, muddy, crying, she was told by her mother to go around the house and use the back door.

What is more precious in our collective biography than those very things which we elect to conceal or discard? Discard is the most enduring version of circulation; discard, not retention, constitutes the materiality of trace.

In her questioning of notions of the unique and singular self, Kleinhart turns often in her work to the slippage between the words "I" and "It." On a sheet of paper in the stack that I have labeled Blue-One she writes, almost confusingly:

He was standing at my back door.
It was late in the afternoon.

By the recording of something that was possibly not in her photographs she permits herself to continue:

> At the back door the assassin
> handed me his knife.
> He asked for a slice of bread.

> At the back door Louis Riel
> asked if he might use the bathroom.

HORNBOOK #76

"Sometimes I hear in my speech traces of languages I don't remember knowing."

This preposterous statement is scrawled on a scrap of paper somewhere in the stack I have labeled Red-Two. And yet one thinks not only of Indo-European roots, but also of the impossible moment when somewhere, somehow, a speaker joined together—let us say—three words.

Kleinhart claimed to be writing investigative poems. What, pray tell, was she investigating?

She writes not once but twice, each time as if for the first time:

The river of no flows over us.
Nothing is new.

[in one of the two versions the word surprise is
written over the word no, but neither word is scratched
out]

I confess to puzzlement. Frankly, you would have
to lie down flat on your back in the Battle River to have
the water flow over you. The huge valley of that river
was not carved out by the piddling stream that it now
contains; the outwash of retreating glaciers created
what now seems a pastoral site.

Rita Kleinhart was not one to look for connec-
tions.

Sometimes, it seems to me, she thought of people
as some sort of computer virus that had got into the
intelligence of the world. Immediately after her twice-
repeated couplet she writes once:

"When I was a child my Aunt Agnes told me not
to swallow cherry stones. If I swallowed a cherry stone,
she told me, a cherry tree would grow out of my belly.
I shuddered at the idea. And yet I found it curiously
exciting. Growing up in Alberta, I had never seen a
cherry tree."

I would speculate that she had in fact somewhere seen a reproduction of a woodcut from an old book, and in that reproduction a cherry tree cramped into a small, rectangular space. I have seen such reproductions myself. She, however, went on to reckon that her language was freighted with no end of traces that were neither literal nor metaphoric. What in hell, then, I would like to have asked her, were they?

HORNBOOK #61

Rita Kleinhart was at work on a huge—and I would say, bizarre—work that ultimately, I am persuaded, caused her disappearance. She held to the conviction that she might so write her poems that she would leave each object or place or person that fell under her attention undisturbed.

Granted, she did not, looking at back doors, tug at latches or twist at knobs. And yet she proposed at one point in one of her notes (though she may have later abandoned the idea) that she would limit her investigation to her own township. A township is, of course, in its own curious way, a box. Kleinhart has nothing to say on this matter. Or, if the handwriting on sheet #3 in Yellow-Four is hers, then she says unfairly, "A township is not a box."

I should explain to the unwary reader that a township, as conceived in Kleinhart's home province, is a square of land measuring six miles by six miles, resulting in a grid made up of thirty-six squares of land each measuring one mile by one mile. These thirty-six sections (as they are called) are numbered from one to thirty-six, beginning not from the top left-hand corner as one might expect, but rather from the lower right-hand corner, then to the left, then up a row and to the right, then up a row and to the left, then up a row and to the right, in the time-honored manner of a farmer plowing a field with oxen or even with a four-horse team.

Rita Kleinhart went too far, I feel, both with her notions of the nondevelopmental nature of the individual artist's work and with her commitment to versions of the serial.

"Things happen," she writes, "and then things happen. And there is sweet fuck all else to it."

Ideas of development, Rita Kleinhart insisted, make for a false narrative of what it is to be poet or person; as a result the house that survived her disappearance is a hodgepodge of so many midden heaps. And I am stuck with the task of being mild philosopher to her estrangement from both the reality of now and the larger intentions of immortality. Being in-between, she should have realized, we cannot ever be.

Rita and I were lovers for four years. During that time we met three times. Because we were separated in age by a good ten years, I was gone from the Battle River country and launched into my own career by the time she published her first poems.

I did, however, continue to correspond with Rita after our unfortunate separation (though my letters to her are, so far, not to be found in her house). In one of her letters she tells me, "If you are going to appropriate from your own life, do so with immense care."

By way of retort I penned her a three-line stanza:

Retreating from his own back door
the invisible man stepped on his invisible dog
and, having been bitten, bled red blood.

Her sullen little response was to send me a postcard saying what I had already understood: "Listen. Raymond. If you are going to . . ." Et cetera. Et cetera.

At that point I became a bit huffy. I told her, by special delivery, in no uncertain terms, that I would prefer to be left out of her collective biography.

She responded by writing me a pair of three-line stanzas for which I can only assume I was the inspiring if invisible muse:

At the back door of the CN boxcar
the immigrant farmer ate the horse
he had intended to ride home.

At the back door of the homestead shack
the immigrant wife called to her husband,
Where did you pack the wine-dark sea?

I suppose it was unfair of me to be flip in my response, but I responded by writing, "I see you would like to see me again."

Her response was a long and remarkably clumsy sentence that struck something of a blow at her collective biography:

"The loneliness of the poet is so immense I might only endure it by sending you blank postcards from the museum of your mind."

HORNBOOK #43

Rita thought of calling her book *Chance of Flurries.*

That she elected not to is fortunate, since I would surely propose other titles for her unfinished magnum opus.

We write as a way of inviting love. Each text is a request that says, please, love me a little.

Rita Kleinhart was an admirer of snow. Snow, she remarks, is the caress of impossible meanings. Snow is closure without ending.

Snow is the veil that lets us see the shape of the dream. Rita left two solitary lines in the stack of papers I have labeled Blue-One:

A skiff of snow, this morning, rides the stubble sun.
The gosling, holding madly still, accounts the gun.

I, too, have walked in the ribald dark, asking forgiveness. In the absence of the gun, snow suffices.

What is the heart but the muscular, thick skin of an abiding secret?

She referred to me as the intrigued lover.

Broken, she said, and wrote these lines after that solitary word, as if she had put down a title:

He is the intrigued lover who loves first
his own hands. His hands betray my nipples.
His hands are scissors that break rocks.
And yet he is the intrigued lover who asks,
Where do you go when you close your eyes?

Only three lines later, she, for some reason, changes the abiding pronoun:

You of the stalled orgasm, fearing an end—
I give you nothing. Die by your own hand.
Love is a pleasure of the mouth. Eat your words.

Surely she intends these final lines for me. She is nothing if not direct. I see in these lines intimations of her disappearance; what is love but a disappearing act that leaves the beholder staggering in blind pursuit? I find Rita nowhere, and yet I am in her arms when I awaken. She ties me to my bed.

Her restless words begin, like the hot lick of snow, their incisions.

HORNBOOK #65

I wrote to her and said, Say hello to Zero, but she wrote back and said, We met a long time ago, but you don't remember. That's when I replied, I love you, but how would you know?

> *A drunken angel fell upon the chimneys of the town.*
> *A woman in a doorway heard a weeping.*
> *She said it was the whimsy of a clown.*

Did Rita write those exquisite lines, or did I?

I have always admired Li Po and Tu Fu. I think of that drunk man—Li Po?—seeing the moon in the water and believing he saw the figured, white, round, smooth, cloven, irresistible ass of his love. He reached to offer a kiss. He would embrace what most he desired. I once sent Rita a postcard reminding her of the event. Even now I weep small tears of my own at Li Po's drowning.

Poet, before I forget, tell me nothing.

HORNBOOK #94

"fragments after a fragment." That would be my title for her work. I once wrote to Rita, telling her as much.

She wrote in reply: "'Headset' would be the proper

title for your own speculations. Your way of not hearing the noise. You put on your headset and you hear one sound with determined exactness."

She was surely and ever the champion of background noise, a fact that makes her disappearance into silence all the more irritating. Was not her life on a ranch silence enough?

I am reminded of a couplet she sent me shortly after we entered into what was to be a correspondence, and I had the temerity to say our beginning to correspond was a good thing:

Your life broke its leg;
you ought to shoot it.

"Gibberish," I replied.

"Precisely," she wrote back. "Now you are beginning to here."

HORNBOOK #48

I am reminded of a comment from the bleared, hazel eyes of old _____ : "Autobiography is not memory."

Apart, we hold hands. Our bodies become the signs of what it is they want to deny. Only our bodies are unable to forget. Sometimes when I look at the paintings in her living room, she is at my side.

In the first two stanzas Rita stands at her back door, guessing where she might put a new birdhouse. She admired the chickadees of winter.

The track of the swallow is certain but unpredictable. Dismembered, the poem assures itself: hold on there.

"Now where did that garden get to?" Rita asks at the end of Hornbook #48.

HORNBOOK #29

We read flatly what cannot be flat. The open prairie conceals a chasm. How does one dare walk through tall grass?

Surprise, surprise.
It was surprise put out his eyes.

I quote. But I would like to propose my own substitution for Rita's offending lines:

The gopher, standing up to see,
gets shot between the eyes.

HORNBOOK #30

Why do I imagine phone calls in which she tells me
I have disappeared?

HORNBOOK #4

The hornbook is itself a book, but a book one
page in length. Framed and wearing a handle, covered
in transparent horn, it sets out to fool no one. It says
its say. Rita Kleinhart seems not to have got a handle
on this realization. What she claimed for her poems
was exactly that which they did not provide: the clarity
of the exact and solitary and visible page. The framed
truth, present and unadorned. Not a page for the turning, no, but rather the poem as relentless as a mirror
held in the hand. The framed and confident statement,
announcing precept or command; the framed list, offering the barest alphabet and numerals of our lives. A
one-page book covered in horn, but not a horny book.
The dehorned beast, offering its last sign and protec-
tion to protect the isolate sheet of paper and its insistent economy of words.

HORNBOOK #22

I once phoned Rita to say I feel safe only when on airplanes.

I make my living as a courier—or, as I prefer to say, using a word that refuses to wear a disguise, messenger. I deliver confidential documents from place to place, from continent to continent.

While up in the sky I write a few poems of my own. Or I used to. Of course I could not afford to let them survive any landing. Let me tell you, a messenger recognized as a poet would soon be out of business.

"Writing," Rita assured me in her absurd way, "is not about delivering messages." She dotted in an ellipsis as if to give me time to think. "It is equally important," she went on, "that we have messengers and keep them desperately busy. Do you know what I mean?"

Since Rita left her Alberta ranch at best once a month, and usually to travel something under two hundred kilometers, she was hardly in a position to deliver messages to anyone.

Hornbook #22 contains the curious lines:

crushed red shale in my lane,
rain falling on fallen rain on
crushed red shale, fire, flood

The long lane that leads from the paved road to her ranch house is indeed covered with crushed red shale. Saskatoons and chokecherries grow in patches here and there, along the lane. Pasture sage finds a place in the bunch grass. Wild roses. A slough with its ring of willows and trembling aspen. But what one sees mostly and simply is barns, granaries, corrals, a ranch house that is at once rambling and severely unprotected, there on a stretch of prairie overlooking the wide valley of the Battle River.

"Where would I go?" she asked me, when I asked why she didn't travel.

Her disappearance, while in the Frankfurt Museum of Modern Art, puzzles her enemies and friends alike. I have never told anyone that I am certain I saw her late one afternoon on a Singapore subway train, only eight months after her disappearance. She, of course, gave me not so much as a blink of recognition. Seeing her as I did, through a moving window, I was reminded of her photographs of back doors—photos in which, by accident, she more than once captured herself as a reflection in glass.

Why did I not try to overtake her, there in Singapore? Quite simply because I respect her wish to remain silent.

During that same trip, while on a 747 returning home from London, I wrote in response to Hornbook #22:

She is poet to her own patience.
She rides the long hours, rounding up
strayed words. Howdy, pardner.

HORNBOOK #23

Can there be a poetics of regret? Not likely. Rather, I find in Rita's work a longing for the future. This longing is not in any way utopian. Nor does it hint of a longing for death—which is only a curious variant of the utopian. Her disappearance, rather, had everything to do with entrance into the world. Only by disappearing could she escape the bonded ghost she had become to her few readers. By that act of disappearing—and I believe she willed it—she gave freedom to her poems. And further, she freed herself of any need to write more poems. Her existing poems could begin the process of rewriting themselves, as any poems must that are to be felt as poems.

Rita writes a mere two lines [see the variant version of Hornbook #23 in the stack of papers labeled Yellow-Three—she left those lines out of the published version] on the subject of air travel, and yet those same lines anticipate my entire life. I am destined never to land. I am confined to air. I am the prisoner of flight. Rita, unwittingly, anticipated my fate.

She would seem in those gifted lines to anticipate a kind of love for me. I can only say, now that she is absent, that I, too, loved her.

I think of myself, often, while circling around this little planet, as flying around her, always toward her. I carry with me her small sheaf of poems. I read them and am compelled by their knotted intentions into words of my own.

Now she has taken flight and I am alone in the sky.

HORNBOOK #66

"I have to run around and pick a few things up."

The last time I dropped by to see her on her secluded ranch, I found the above note nailed to the back door. Rita made an adventure of driving her pick-up into town. She could hardly have anticipated that I might drive two hours from the city in order to share with her a pot of coffee. That she did not feel it necessary to scrawl my name on the message is further evidence of her assumption of our connection.

Poetry itself is just such a surmise. I speak to no one, knowing you will recognize that I speak to you.

HORNBOOK #67

Rita, shortly after her disappearance, began to send back to her ranch house postcards addressed to herself. At least, I am certain it was she who sent them, this deduction based on their content.

"It was my every intention . . ." she wrote, addressing herself. And then, hardly a week later, she sent herself a message that she must have assumed would fall into my hands: "What are you flying off about?" she asks, on the back of a card that pictures a large jet with nothing behind it but sky.

Both cards bear French stamps. Both arrived hardly a month after the provincial authorities named me as the person to take responsibility for the handling of her literary papers. The law recognized that our love relationship had continued, even if that recognition was beyond Rita herself.

HORNBOOK #7

"I am attempting to write an autobiography in which I do not appear."

Rita Kleinhart, in making this comment on her own poem—a comment I found attached to the manuscript of the final (and published) version of Hornbook #7—both announces and betrays the posture that is the very bedrock of her entire poetic sequence.

She would, so to speak, deny her own signature. And yet she wore the world in a way that was uniquely hers. She loved the smell of a shared bedroom, the distant calling of cows and calves, the taste of swollen raspberries made wet with fresh cream—even if she claimed not to love me.

HORNBOOK #8

Rita is painfully absent when I let myself in at the back door of her richly modest home.

"A man of your age. For shame," she once commented, while we were in the throes of our lovemaking. I had, while kissing her back, quietly slipped her jeans well down below her waist and let my tongue in at the cleavage of her perfect behind.

A man of my age, indeed. I was precisely a decade her senior. She and I became lovers on her fiftieth birthday. I was, at the time, sixty years of age.

Is not poetry a questing after place, a will to locate? I fly, and I weary of flight. Rita was mistaken when she speculated that I take to the sky under the fond illusion that I might in that manner get nearer the sun.

We were talking.

"Do you like it?"

"Yes."

We were talking.

HORNBOOK #3

"How is it," the poet asks herself in Blue-One, "that the poet writing writes herself into the recognition that she is not saying what she wishes to say?"

Recognizing this, the poet moves on, doesn't she? Death follows after like a dumb admirer. What is the poetic function of the hand?

Once upon a time, long ago.
Long a time. Once upon a go.
Long upon ago a once a time.
A time ago upon. A long. A once.

I was trying to tell you a story, Rita. I had troubled getting stopped.

Lugubrious as love,
we love.

HORNBOOK #39

As a small child I was puzzled by clocks. I studied the face of the large clock mounted on the wall in our kitchen, and I tried to understand how adults looked at that face and then said to each other: "The train is late today." "The roast should be done by now." "It's time the children took their baths."

The face of the clock was a hieroglyphic I could

not penetrate. I studied the slow pointing of the hands from number to number. I had learned the numerals well enough so that I might read them up to twelve. But how did those numerals tell people to wash their faces and comb their hair? How did that circle of motionless numbers tell people to say good-bye to each other and to go out into the dark and the cold of the night?

HORNBOOK #40

"Discomfort," Rita told me, and this over a breakfast of ham and eggs and brown toast and her own homemade chokecherry jelly, "is what you look for in a poem, Raymond. You seek discomfort the way you seek dislocation."

By way of smart retaliation—and our fingers touched across her kitchen table as I spoke—I quoted from her own Hornbook #39:

Home is a door that opens inward only.
"So how will you get out, stranger?" I say
to myself.

"Perhaps I was only suggesting," she said, smiling mischievously, "that words are a lock, not a key."

"Then how do you explain," I said, not smiling at all, "that every time I peek in at your keyhole, I get a shiner?"

"Who is this I?" she asked.

"Your own Raymond."

"I can't place him."

"I think he loves you," I said. "He's probably hiding somewhere in this house."

HORNBOOK #77

"The poets of Canada learn to sing by walking barefoot on gravel beaches. This makes for a fascinated listening. A constricted listening."

Why did she not speak of the writing? But no, not Rita—she, the poet, would speak of the listening instead.

I'm not convinced she ever heard a word I spoke to her. I offered her praise and love. She did not know how to accept either. We deceive ourselves into words when all that cries out is the body, wanting touch and taste and smell and sight. Do you hear me?

Words are the fake pockets on a new jacket. You cannot tumble into one of them so much as a token coin. Words are what we are left with by the bird that hits the window.

Invisibility was what Rita wanted. I asked her on a May afternoon what she would like for her birthday. "An eraser," she said.

"My dear," I replied. "I am offering you all of me."

You see, until Rita Kleinhart chose to disappear there in Frankfurt, I thought of myself as a poet. That I wrote the poems while in the air, that I destroyed them just before the plane's tires smoked down onto gray pavement, has nothing to do with what I knew I was doing. I was a poet. It was my touching the delete button that made those high poems complete. What I might dredge up from memory now, in order to communicate with Rita's absence, has nothing to do with the poems as they existed in the clear sky. Every published poem is its own elegy. What poet is not astonished, reading the mere poem on the mere page? The mere transcription of that other poem onto paper is a calamity, a desecration. Every poem, one might say, is a failed translation, an accidental impostor manu-fractured by the incompetence of a weak-eyed translator sweating in the light of a lantern whose wick is badly in need of a trimming. The wind blows hard. The flame flickers. The sooty globe needs a wiping. The word asshole comes to mind. And, yes, after flying across continents and oceans, while approaching once again this petty, stinking earth, while ignoring some stewardess or other who cries out incoherent commands, I have rushed at the very last minute to the john at the back of the plane, pushed my way into a filthy cubicle (and during a flight of eight hours the human mob declares itself by its telltale toilet inscriptions to be what it is) and there proffered the scribbly copies of my absolute poems to the sudden, loud suck and the whoosh and the exquisite oblivion of the Teflon shitter.

HORNBOOK #19

Rita was accustomed to the deceptive randomness of wind and rain and sky, to the violence and the blinding inevitability of prairie sun. She had an aversion to intentional space.

She wrote on page three of the stack of notes I have labeled Blue-Two:

"A patch of scarlet mallow appears each spring in the grasses on the edge of the coulee directly in front of my house. That little patch of orange-red blossoms, emerging on a dry, south-facing slope, is one of my reasons for living."

She wrote on page nine of Blue-Two:

"I have discovered that negligence is a gifted gardener."

Forgive me for scribbling on the bottom of that same page nine (and I was a boy when my mother died; Rita's mother lived to see her daughter celebrated as a poet):

"The day they brought my mother's body home to our house for the wake, I went up the low hill behind the house. Rita, I wanted to tell you this. I went to a hollow beside a large round rock, and I curled up in that hollow and I cried until I had cried out my life. After that I was empty enough to be a writer. I returned to the house and went to my room and made a list of the names of the neighbors who came with food and flowers."

There in Frankfurt, on the occasion of Rita's disappearance (and I was standing beside her in that darkened room where one believes one is looking at a painting only to discover, as one's eyes adjust to the dark, that one is staring into a faintly lit recession set blankly into a blank wall), I turned to remark that I found James

Turrell's "Twilight Arch" compelling nevertheless, for all the absence of an image. I turned and she was not there.

"In the end, we are defeated by gardens. They know too much." This is a fragment (see Blue-Two, page twenty-four) she chose not to include in Hornbook #19.

HORNBOOK #44

[an endnote to begin with: Rita felt little need to travel in this ravaged world. She once heard me speak of the city of Coimbra in Portugal and (if I am not mistaken) wrote Hornbook #44 in response to my claiming to have shed tears at the sound of a voice I heard without ever laying eyes on the singer.]

1

I am happy in the Coimbra night.
The stars feed on the carrion of our lives.
There where the mountains break and fall
the city dreams a fatal song.

2

The castle at the end of the curled road
sings fado. The pale trees weep leaves,

offering embrace to stone.
I become the voice I hear.

3

The lemon tree by the window wears
two birds. The birds are not singing.
I listen to their song.
Why is the fountain crying?

4

The woman in the bus who sang
sang softly of our long delay.
We were going nowhere.
I drank the song the woman sang.

5

You were as strange as love.
The fado bar was empty,
except for all of us.
There in Coimbra, I listen.

[I hardly need explain that Rita here misrepresents me badly. (Not to mention her inability to live in either the present or the past.) I had delivered a package of documents to a wine merchant in Oporto and while there decided I would take the train south to Coimbra, largely because I was told of a shop that had on sale some rare green tiles. It was not my intention to listen in on any fado. I might add that by the time I got to the tile shop the objects of my little quest were gone.]

HORNBOOK #46

[Kleinhart was a compelled poet. She disappeared into art.]

"Raymond," Rita told me one afternoon while we were eating ripe peaches on the deck outside her kitchen door, "if urine came forth as song, you'd still manage to remain silent."

"Give me a little credit," I said. "At least I try not to be a poet."

I asked her what she looked for in a man and she said she looked for signs of fair play. "Pass me that knife," she added. She had a way of splitting a peach with a knife, then removing the stone. I prefer to eat the stone free of the sweet-smelling flesh.

She had a way of remembering everything I made

the mistake of saying. Men can't talk, she liked to tell me. "Let me tell you about it," I said, trying to see her through the screen door that opened onto the deck. I had stepped into the kitchen to find a bottle opener. She snapped a picture of me through the screen.

Rita fancied herself a recluse. She lived alone in her ranch house and leased her land to neighboring ranchers. The mailman once told me when I asked him if he had seen her leave that the mailbox where her driveway joined the gravel road was sometimes stuffed full to overflowing before she deigned to empty it.

When I complained, licking the peach juice from the fingers of my right hand, that she almost never wrote me a letter, she explained that she allowed herself to write one letter and one only each week, no matter what urgencies might surround her.

"Embrace," I suggested. "Not surround."

"Surround," she said.

He is become the belled cat,
I the mouse, rosy and fat.

HORNBOOK #47

This hornbook is one of the two hornbooks bearing the subtitle, Exhibit A. In the middle of an otherwise rational poem she speculates:

When one has had one's say, assay
Or not at all the bed to climb

Do not attend the buttoned if
of once and then the truly stiff

The lowly page and laughter rhyme
the pubic tale itself bewray

The tousled straw with love acquaint
The tasseled town a red to paint

Surely we recognize in these unlikely lines her intention to erase herself from the literary scene. She is, here, as good as gone. A goner. She abjures sense as we think we know it. She tells us there is another possibility in language and she is on her way to ask what it is. She adds on a postcard apparently intended for herself but never mailed, "Some days poetry is a dialogue with nobody."

"Raymond," she assured me, when I inquired about

the Exhibit A thing, "there is more than meets the eye standing between well hung and well hanged."

HORNBOOK #57

I suppose it's time I commented on Rita's famous little verse that the literary folk like to refer to as "I'm So Glad You Called":

I'm so glad you called, asshole, the house was
pleasantly quiet before the phone rang and you
tried to say hello, hello, you said, as if even
the door frame should remember your final
good-bye. Hey, good-bye. I'm so glad you called.

Hardly an auspicious opening. I wish someone would praise me for my ironic reply:

O once my heart was full of joy,
but now it's full of song instead.
Who was it wronged this singing boy?
What was it done me wrong in bed?

And why is it that only pain can make us burst into words? Did Rita trump up her occasional rejections of me just so that I might be given the power of speech?

We went head to head as poets, she and I, there's no denying it. She was into that willful stuff. The old forms were good enough for me, and on occasion I now take one of her poems and give it the look it should have by finding in her disorder a quatrain or two. I once asked her what done me wrong and she replied, "Try who, Raymond."

What small perversions of the body make us sing? Tickled in the groin, we giggle poems. Fuck it.

The aging apple and the angled ache.
O blaggard laggard line, indeed. Opaque.

HORNBOOK #51

What did she see in me? I ask you. And let me answer my own question before you make a wrong guess. She saw in me the aging lover who made her ever young. She saw in me the silence that must speak itself by quoting her. She heard in me tra-la tra-la.

As poets we attribute to ourselves the poems we record on paper. The presumption of the poet is one of technology's petty triumphs.

Should we not say that every poem is "attributed"

to the poet named in small print under the title? What rapacious need makes the poet claim the multitude by the small ordering of a signature?

Does it not take a bundle of texts, a blather of lives, to blunder one poem out of one isolate and acquisitive poet?

Poetry is excrement. It is marginally useful as fertilizer. In using it as fertilizer we run the risk of transmitting a variety of venereal diseases.

Rita Kleinhart saw in me the klutz who might bumble her obscurity into the annals—and why not anals?—of that morbidity we call literature.

What torpor is it that enables the poet to drowse a few scribbles onto the beauty of a white page?

Is not the elegance of almost any naked ass to be preferred to the puffy regurgitation of accumulated consonants?

Kick a dong of lickpence,
A belly full of blear.

It is high time we got down to the text.

HORNBOOK #52

I wonder sometimes if Rita is in this house where I, in her absence, am supposed to be ordering her papers. What if her apparent disappearance was a clever way of luring me into her home?

Sometimes, late at night, I swear I hear footsteps. Poetry is a radical form of stealth. What does that make of the poet?

Sometimes, I swear, her papers, come morning, are not exactly where I left them the previous night. Something I could not track down late at night is there in the morning, obvious, staring me in the face.

To take poetry into one's hands is to take one's own life into one's hands. Surely Rita understood this when she asked me, late one evening, if I would, should the need arise, organize her papers and have them deposited in the vaults of the University of Calgary Special Collections Library. When I told her next morning that, yes, I would be happy to oblige, she asked me what I was talking about.

Hornbook #52 makes mention of a ghost that Rita claimed was somehow herself; when she caught glimpses of its presence in her sprawling house, there on the edge of the Battle River coulees, she had the sensation that the ghost, not she, was Rita Kleinhart.

Why do I listen so intently, in the dark, to the small winds that walk up out of the river valley? One midnight I woke with a start at the touch of a hand to my throat, and found the hand was my own. We are never safe from ourselves, never. We stave off that marauder, the marauder who writes the poem, by writing the poem.

HORNBOOK #24

"Sometime," Rita said, "I want to go all the way up to the tree line."

We were hiking together, into the bare, south-facing coulee hills to the west of the ranch. I helped Rita take off her hiking boots and her socks. I kissed the blisters on the bottoms of her toes. As I knew on my lips the changing taste of her sweat I knew I had strayed from her toes to her ankles, then from her ankles to the backs of her knees, then from the sweaty backs of her knees to her inner thighs. She said, at the edge of my hearing, "All I can see is empty sky."

211

Lying on my belt buckle, facing east, all I could see was the bush of her body.

"Bush," I whispered.

HORNBOOK #81

antiquarian apes arrange ancestors
bees brush berries' bosoms
crimped clowns cuddle catastrophes

These unfortunate lines are to be found in the heap of Rita's abandoned papers I have labeled Yellow-Three. These lines did not make their way into any of her poems. She scribbled on at length.

dutiful dotards delight dowagers
entrancing enemas entertain enemies
farthest friends forget favors

One cannot help but detect a message even in scraps so random as these doodled lines. I am hardly to be judged paranoid if I hear in these fragments a fore-dooming of my simple joy. Rita loved to hate me. Forgive the cliché, but there it is, and the devil take the hindmost, what are words but unavoidable accidents? You must practice, she told me, and this in no uncertain terms, to confound the possibility of your encountering your own double.

We think we think. That's what I think.

HORNBOOK #82

You are what remains after night's fall.
You are what remains after nights fail.

I check her phone bills for calling card charges, then pay up out of my own pocket, since most of the calls are apparently my own. I try to remember her last words, there in the museum in Frankfurt. We had not spoken for a considerable time before I turned to break the silence and found she was not there at my side. Perhaps she said to me, "You should drink your apple juice, it will relieve your anxiety about your bowel movements." But that was before I fell into my sulk, and I had, yes, fallen into a little sulk; but she knew I like my times of quiet, times inevitably followed by chatter and stark need. Perhaps she said to me, "How can you do this, travel for a living, entering into languages of which you understand not a word?" But those were not her final words, she would not let the matter rest there, be assured. We were having an early breakfast at an outdoor restaurant in front of a row of restored houses, in some sort of a square, and at the time we were talking about architecture. I had become a bit owlish before she said, "You are the prisoner of space, not I, Raymond. And please, if nothing else, I beg you, drink your apple juice." I think she had something more to say. Perhaps my truculence silenced her. We marched off in silence together toward the renowned museum.

It is in Hornbook #82 that she writes:

Final words are as good a place as any;
having begun, we dare to begin

As I say, and let me repeat, I cannot for the life of me recall what her final words might have been. She did send postcards that day, the day of her celebrated disappearance. But none to me. And did she perchance have the cards written and addressed before she conned me into a petty disagreement about who is the prisoner and of what, and how does a shared language do anything but seal tight the door on its rusty hinges? Rap rap, we say, knocking our knuckles red. Hello? Is there anyone home?

That her house has only a minimal attic is a shame; even a ghost in Rita Kleinhart's attic would find itself homeless.

HORNBOOK #49

"Some days I have nothing to do," I once told Rita, "and can't find the time to get it done."

"Sometimes," Rita replied, "waking up in the morning is like falling asleep."

That is why I do not now believe she disappeared when she disappeared. By her lascivious feigning she turned me into the merest lackey who must propagate her poems.

I, the drear and monkey-slave of time;
she, eternal spinner of sublime.

I, scrawny, the dancer at her feet;
she the grinder grinding out the beat.

She, continuous, like god, or scat,
sets me upon the ground to pass her hat.

Let me, my dearest dear, add my own two cents' worth. One would like to assume that even a poet, a poet feigning death, a poet proclaiming the untoward liberty of her poems, might recollect the oblong press of desire.

Tickle tickle little tum.
How I wonder where you bum.

So there.

Acknowledgments

This is (not) an autobiography. These fugitive pieces, with only minor exceptions, are concerned with the writing life, not with the personal life, of the writer.

◈

"Why I Went Up North and What I Found When I Got There." Annual Conference of the Association for Canadian Studies in The German Speaking Countries, Grainau, Germany, 24 February 1989.

"Why I Went Up North and What I Found When I Got There." *Zeitschrift der Gesellschaft für Kanada-Studien.* Eds. Kurt Jurgensen and Jans-Josef Niedere-

he. Neumunster: Karl Wachholz Verlag, 1989.
39–50.

Martin Kuester, who teaches at the University of Augsburg, was instrumental in persuading me to give the talk in Grainau that serves as the introductory essay. The writing of this talk gave me the notion of assembling a collection of pieces on my writing life. I am further and in various ways indebted to John and Barbara Thieme; they gave me the leisure, in their home and at the University of Hull (October 1993) to explore the mystery of a possible table of contents.

✛

"I Wanted to Write a Manifesto." The Marjorie Ward Lecture, St. John's College, University of Manitoba, 17 November 1989.

Professor Jeanne Delbaere, in Brussels, invited me to present this same essay at a conference she organized at her university, this with the recognition that a different audience would hear a different story.

"I Wanted to Write a Manifesto." Multiple Voices: Recent Canadian Fiction: Lvth International Symposium, Université Libre de Bruxelles, Bruxelles, Belgium, 29 November 1989. Published in *Multiple*

Voices: Recent Canadian Fiction. Ed. Jeanne Delbaere. Australia/Denmark/U.K.: Dangeroo Press, 1990. 7–21.

✦

"The Cow in the Quicksand and How I(t) Got Out: Responding to Stegner's *Wolf Willow.*" Common Ground: Eighth Annual Literary Conference of the Manitoba Writers' Guild, Winnipeg, Manitoba, 12 October 1989. Published in *Border Crossings* 10.1 (Jan 1991): 56–62. Also in *Beyond Borders: An Anthology of New Writing from Manitoba, Minnesota, Saskatchewan and the Dakotas.* Eds. Mark Vinz and Dave Williamson. New Rivers/Turnstone Press, 1992. 129–143.

✦

Books referred to in the Quicksand essay:

Butala, Sharon. *The Gates of the Sun.* Saskatoon: Fifth House, 1985.

Cooley, Dennis. *Leaving.* Winnipeg: Turnstone Press, 1980.

Stegner, Wallace, *Wolf Willow: a History, a Story, and a*

Memory of the Last Plains Frontier. 1955. New York: The
Viking Press, Viking Compass Edition, 1967.

✦

"Playing Dead" was presented as an after-dinner talk on
     29 September 1992, at the Fifth Interdisciplinary
     Symposium on Western Canada & Europe, Winnipeg,
     Manitoba. The title of the Symposium was "Kanadis-
     tik–Centre and Periphery." Professor Herbert Zirker
     was the retiring originator of the Trier–Manitoba
     University Partnership. Rudy Wiebe's book *Playing
     Dead: A Contemplation Concerning the Arctic* was published
     by NeWest Press (Edmonton, 1989).

✦

"Lonesome Writer Diptych" is my third attempt at
     telling the story of my father's watch. We are, occa-
     sionally, obsessed by seemingly minor incidents that
     speak to us secretly in a major way. I first examined
     the incident in a talk ("Taking Apart My Father's
     Watch: The Case for Canadian Writing") I gave in
     1991 on the campus of the University of Coimbra,
     Coimbra, Portugal, at the invitation of Roger
     Ramalhete and Carole Galaise. That talk was pub-

lished in *O CÂNONE NOS ESTUDOS ANGLO-AMERI-CANOS.* Ed. Isabel Caldeira. Coimbra: Livraria Minerva, 1994. 67–75. I reconsidered—or recontex-tualized—the incident in "Dancing With The Time Machine, or, Where Are You From?" *The Road Home: New Stories from Alberta Writers.* Ed. Fred Stenson. Edmonton: Reidmore Books Inc, 1992. 297–301.

◆

The poem "Family Reunion Cowboy Poem" was com-posed to be performed 1 July 1994, Community Hall, Heisler, Alberta. We were a gathering of nearly 300 people, the descendants and spouses and conse-quent generations of Lorenz Kroetsch and Theresia Tshirhart, who moved from Waterloo County, Ontario, to Bruce County, Ontario, in the early 1860s, in order to find a new site for a watermill. They built their watermill south of Formosa, on the Teeswater River. Their two children, Ambrose and Henry, went west to homestead.

◆

"D-Day and After: Remembering a Scrapbook I Cannot Find" was presented as a talk in conjunction with the Homecoming of the Class of 1944 at the University of Manitoba, 16 September 1994.

✦

David Staines of the University of Ottawa invited me to give the talk "Sitting Down to Write" on Margaret Laurence at "The Margaret Laurence Symposium," Reappraisals: Canadian Writers, University of Ottawa, 1 May 1994. In preparing the talk I discovered again how profoundly *The Diviners* speaks a poetics of prose fiction.

✦

"Poem for My Dead Sister" appeared in *West Coast Line*, 5 (25/2) Fall 1991.

✦

I read the opening hornbooks of "The Poetics of Rita Kleinhart" at the conference "Inglish: Writing with an Accent," Western Front, Vancouver, 20–21 November 1992. Roy Miki was the organizer of that event.

Four of the hornbooks from "The Poetics of Rita Kleinhart" appeared in *West Coast Line*, 10 (27/1) Spring 1993.

A considerable part of "The Poetics of Rita Kleinhart" appeared in *Open Letter*, Ninth Series, Number 2, Spring 1995, thanks to Susan Rudy Dorscht and Frank Davey.

I am indebted to Dennis Johnson and Nicole Markotic of Red Deer College Press for their patience and their plotting. Nicole Markotic is the secret agent of the Press; Dennis Johnson is the genius loci of a landscape that contains within itself a publisher.

About the Author

ROBERT KROETSCH is one of Canada's most original and respected authors and literary theorists. He was born and raised on a homestead near Heisler, Alberta, and studied at the Universities of Alberta and Iowa. Until the late 1970s, he taught literature and creative writing at the State University of New York. Having recently retired from teaching at the University of Manitoba, his writing continues to influence the direction of Canadian literature. During his career, which spans almost fifty years, he has lectured in Canada, the United States and Europe. Among his more than twenty books are *The Studhorse Man* (Governor General's Award, 1969), *The Stone Hammer Poems, Seed Catalogue, The Sad Phoenician, Field Notes, Badlands, The Words of My Roaring, What the Crow Said, Excerpts From the Real World, The Lovely Treachery of Words* and *The Puppeteer*.